GENDER
AND FAMILY THERAPY

Charlotte Burck & Gwyn Daniel

Foreword by
Virginia Goldner

Systemic Thinking and Practice Series
Series Editors
David Campbell & Ros Draper

London
KARNAC BOOKS

This edition first published in 1995 by
H. Karnac (Books) Ltd.
58 Gloucester Road
London SW7 4QY

Copyright © 1995 by Charlotte Burck and Gwyn Daniel

The rights of Charlotte Burck and Gwyn Daniel to be identified as authors of this work have been asserted in accordance with §§ 77 and 78 of the Copyright Design and Patents Act 1988.

All rights reserved. No part of this publication may be reproduced, stored in a retrieval system, or transmitted in any form or by any means, electronic, mechanical, photocopying, recording or otherwise, without the prior permission of the publisher.

British Library Cataloguing in Publication Data

Burck, Charlotte
    Gender and Family Therapy. — (Systemic
Thinking & Practice Series)
I. Title II. Daniel, Gwyn III. Series
616.89156

ISBN 1 85575 072 4

Printed in Great Britain by BPC Wheatons Ltd, Exeter

to

Ben

and

Tamar

ACKNOWLEDGEMENTS

To Gill Gorell Barnes, whose constant encouragement has forced us to value our thinking.

To those who have worked and trained with us and helped sharpen our understanding of gender.

To families we have worked with who have helped us respect its complexities.

CONTENTS

EDITORS' FOREWORD — ix
FOREWORD by Virginia Goldner — xi

Introduction — 1

Chapter one
Gender: a systemic understanding — 9

Chapter two
Feminisms and other "isms" — 21

Chapter three
Gender and subjectivity — 35

Chapter four
Gender, power, and systemic thinking — 49

Chapter five
Abuses of power:
working with physical and sexual violence   63

Chapter six
Stories lived and told: language and discourse   77

Chapter seven
Case studies   89

Chapter eight
Training and supervision: addressing the context of gender 119

Chapter nine
Training exercises   129

Chapter ten
Conclusions and future directions   139

REFERENCES AND BIBLIOGRAPHY   145
INDEX   155

EDITORS' FOREWORD

We believe that the feminist movement and the ensuing debates about gender have made an enormous contribution to the way all of us think about the world in which we live, and as editors we are pleased to present this new book which both clarifies many issues in the debate and moves the debate forward. A book that is on the cutting edge of much of the new thinking in the family therapy field always runs the risk of being out of date by the day of publication. But this Series lends itself well to *Gender and Family Therapy* because the ideas are current and have been published very soon after the authors committed them to paper.

What this book does, very helpfully, is to move gender and power beyond the battlefield of polemics towards the realm of therapy in which such ideas exert a considerable influence on the way therapists see the world and carry out their work. These concepts are converted into therapeutic tools because they are well integrated with therapists' traditional preoccupations such as how to connect with family members, or how to help families change. The authors go a long way towards demythologizing gender and making it very accessible to practitioners by describing many of their own case examples, in which thinking has been transformed into effective therapeutic practice.

Burck and Daniel share the personal meaning that gender holds for them, and the open and enquiring, rather than definitive, style of their writing makes it easy for the reader to grasp their ideas. The authors' handling in the early chapters of the many intellectual conundrums about gender is clear and assured, and through their many citations of other literature in the field they have managed to align this volume with other scholarly works while at the same time ensuring a very readable and practical book.

David Campbell
Ros Draper
London
February 1995

FOREWORD

Virginia Goldner

In the mid-1970s, a friend and feminist fellow-traveller wrote a paper, much quoted in its time, in which she coined the phrase "dissolving the hyphen" in feminist theory and practice. She was talking about the use of a grammatical sign to convey and finesse the problem of the uneasy relationship between Marxism and feminism, as in the phrase "Marxist–feminist," then very much in vogue. Since this was a relation that would soon be called, in another oft-quoted essay, "an unhappy marriage", the dilemmas of this attachment soon faded from view, and it was the marriage, not the hyphen, that was eventually dissolved.

But while Marxism has all but disappeared as a discourse to be reckoned with in feminist theory, the problem of the hyphen remains. This is because feminism has always been intellectually promiscuous—a necessary evil since no single theoretical language can contain its insights, questions, or dilemmas. Thus, it is not surprising that as Marxism has been eclipsed by other theoretical systems that intrigue and beckon, they too have been appropriated into feminism's unlikely couplings—psychoanalytic feminism, feminist post-modernism, and (even) feminist systems theory, to name a relevant few.

Each of these joinings, depending on how the linkage is made, can potentiate or constrain the development of new ideas and understandings. At this juncture, the lessons of history seem to be pointing towards the post-modern view that fresh insights and paradigm shifts are produced by a fateful encounter between ideas, not a marriage. Indeed, many would argue that such marriages—with their attendant name changes and unwieldy hyphenations—have asked too much of the betrothed in terms of smoothing over conflict and contradiction between the parties, thereby obscuring important differences and particularities in favour of a false synthetic amalgam.

Instead of arranging a marriage of disciplines, many weary philosophers now contend that intellectual synergy can best be fostered just by creating a congenial space in which to bring multiple discourses into dialogue—a space where good conversations can flourish, but where no one is obliged to stay the night.

Charlotte Burck and Gwyn Daniel's book shows us how richly productive good conversations can be. They have taken our current crop of favoured ideas and stances—second-order cybernetics, post-modernism, social constructionism, feminism, narrative and discourse theory—added what's best about systems theory (in their words, an interactional understanding and a sensitivity to context, framing, and level)—and then orchestrated a contrapuntal dialogue where each discourse comments on the other, producing newsworthy fresh ideas.

Here, for example, is one of my favourite one-liners, the outcome of a dialogue between feminism and systemic thinking: "we do not always put gender as the highest order of context, but rather that we think about the question: 'Highest order in which context?'"

As someone who works in many theoretical languages both as a translator and interlocutor, I am sure that that wonderful aphorism took years to hatch, the product of a long, deep immersion in the habit of thinking from multiple perspectives. Moreover, when these mixed metaphors have this wonderful effect—to produce what Bateson called "an increment of knowing," it is because the ideas have been lived and used in many ways (it's not just a matter of moving pieces around a chessboard).

The authors make this clear by their choice to write in a jointly personal voice, eschewing the all-purpose invisible narrator who dominates the text by dispensing a "God's-eye-view" of truth. In this book, the reader's relationship to the ideas on the page is always mediated by an awareness that the text was written *by someone in particular*, who went about her thinking in the context of a specific time and place.

This narrative genre, while not specific to feminism, is nevertheless central to its self-identity, viz. the 1960's slogan "the personal is political". This meant, in formal terms, that feminism was *constituted as a reflexive practice*. It was a theory you lived, because it was your life you theorized.

Living feminism's insights meant living in a state of perpetual critique, a plausibility because we were young middle-class women with a lot of free time. But what was truly significant is that when we grew up, we took our politics with us so that feminism grew as we grew. The original, crudely formulated insights have since evolved into a complex discipline, with sub-fields and specialities. Our daughters (and sons) can now learn, in university courses and in therapies that are guided by feminist insights, about gender's hold on them.

Which brings me back to the text at hand. In another of their many elegant and concise turns of phrase, Burck and Daniel speak of therapy in Foucauldian terms, "as a place ... where questions about personhood are raised, and negotiations about identities take place". This characterization formed the basis of Foucault's melancholic conception of therapy as a disciplinary, regulating practice, but as this book shows, therapy can also be a transitional space where identities are questioned and alternative ways of being explored.

The authors theorize this process by highlighting the reflexivity inherent in identity formation: "We tell the stories we live, and live the stories we tell." They then connect this process with the action of psychotherapy:

Therapeutic dialogue can enable people to discover their stories through the telling. At times, change happens *in the telling*, as the experience of becoming a subject in our own story fundamentally alters our relationship to events in which we experienced ourselves as passive. At other times, the importance is not in the telling but in the *reflecting on the story we have told*, which illuminates the impact of that particular form of narrative, that genre, on us. [chapter 6]

While these ideas may seem familiar since many of us have begun to think about therapy as a story-telling forum, this passage takes us past that somewhat lazy analogy by beginning to call our attention to the mental processes by which stories act on the self.

I was moved and edified by the idea that in the act of telling her story a woman begins to collect herself (pun intended), thus finding the subject who was eclipsed inside the victim. Although this powerful process is known to any decent psychotherapist working with trauma, this way of accounting for it constituted one of those "increments of knowing" that are to be found throughout the book.

Moreover, the passage calls attention to an issue of importance for therapists and activists alike: the search for personal agency in the context of victimization. While it is crucial to document the social forces that construct, constrain, and impinge on us, it is also crucial to search for the subject who invariably creates a personal world nonetheless. Victims are also actors in their lives, and therapy should help them own their agency and extend its boundaries.

In their dense and nuanced discussion of how gender's language and discourse possess us, Burck and Daniel give us new analytic tools and creative clinical strategies with which to mobilize women to embark on this search for themselves (and to help men see through the illusion that, unlike women, *they* are coherent, sovereign subjects).

In the process, the authors show us how therapy can foster a stance of critical inquiry towards the truths of one's time and place, especially about what it means to be a man or woman now.

GENDER AND FAMILY THERAPY

Introduction

Gender and power are woven inextricably into the fabric of therapy. However, most therapists see themselves as committed to understanding each individual's or family's unique reality and often find it hard to fit generalizations about power imbalances or gendered patterns into this intimate, private, and complex human encounter. Alongside this, in aiming to help family members improve the ways in which they get on together, many therapists are wary that talking about issues of gender and power might just make things worse!

What happens when we do bring talk about gender and power overtly into the domain of therapy? Attempting to do so has involved rethinking many of the most cherished tenets of family systems approaches to therapy. It has also challenged therapists to question their own understanding of gender and to address the complex ways in which gender and power are played out in the territory of intimate relationships and in therapy.

In this book, we argue that we can most usefully employ feminist analysis and systemic thinking as complementary frameworks to guide our thinking and practice and to explore these issues. However, in many of the debates about feminism and family therapy, we find "systemic thinking" presented as one category and "feminism" as another, which easily leads to a position where these are seen as two incompatible views of the world. Some feminist writers (e.g. James, 1984) have stated that a systemic framework does not allow questions about gender, power, and inequality to be raised at all. Some systems thinkers, on the other hand, have said that feminism is too constrained a position, too passionate and too prescriptive, to be "systemic".

We aim in this book to move beyond what has often been a sterile and ritualized debate in which "systemic thinkers" regard "feminism" as an essentially lineal view, leading consistently to the same conclusions about blame and victimization, and "feminists" believe that looking at interactional patterns inevitably means that oppresser and oppressed, abuser and abused, are treated as equally responsible for their mutual transactions. We present how we interweave gender preoccupations and systemic ideas in our thinking and practice so that we can emerge with a richer and more complex picture of the dilemmas men and women face and present in therapy, supervision, and training. We hope to share our on-going efforts to "re-story" systemic thinking and ourselves as systemic therapists.

It is not our intention to restate the main feminist critiques of family therapy, which we and many others have covered elsewhere. For key papers, see Burck and Daniel (1990), Goldner (1985, 1987), Hare-Mustin (1978), James and MacIntyre (1983), Jones (1990, 1991), Mackinnon and Miller (1987), and Pilalis and Anderton (1986).

The impetus to write this book arose out of a series of conversations we have had over the past nine years on the subject of feminism and systemic approaches. It is interesting to look back at this earlier period and what the questions were that preoccupied us. Then we were asking: "Why do family therapists ignore gender?" "How is it possible that over a decade of feminist challenge, in every area of our personal and political lives, failed to infiltrate a profession that contains many prominent women practitioners and daily deals with issues of gender inequality in family and couples relationships?" At that time we were both family therapy trainees at the Tavistock Clinic and had each chosen to write about feminism and family therapy for our dissertations. To each of us, it seemed as if the other was the only person interested in such issues—or as Bob Dylan put it: "I've been looking all over for somebody like you. Couldn't find nobody, so you'll have to do."

The experience of being pioneers was a heady but also a misleading one. We were never alone. We were and are especially inspired by Virginia Goldner, whose influence has been profound and who consistently refuses to go for simplistic closure on any difficult issue, and by Marianne Walters, whose therapeutic style has been wonderfully energizing. The Feminism and Family Therapy Conferences that took place in 1987 and 1992 have been contexts within which many British family therapists have shared and developed new ideas about feminist approaches and have formed links.

Now as we survey the field, we can see how much it has been transformed. Ever more literature appears in the form of critiques of theory and practice and expositions of a feminist approach to therapy with a range of different problems and client groups, and no self-respecting conference can afford to ignore "gender issues". The context has inevitably changed, but we are still not sure how far feminist positions have been integrated. One example of this is in the field of eating disorders, where most practitioners acknowledge feminist perspectives on the social construction of the ideal female shape, but where most research papers still use gender-neutral terms such as "patient" and fail to refer to gender at all.

We are also struck that, although many people hold the tension between systemic thinking and feminism clearly in their writing and practice as a strength and a source of creativity (Goldner, 1991a; Goldner, Penn, Sheinberg, & Walker, 1990; Jones, 1990, 1991), many feminist thinkers and systemic therapists continue to stereotype each other's position. We are always interested to see how "feminists" are viewed in the field. Although we think there is now a multiplicity of ways of being a feminist and a systemic therapist, we notice how often feminism is portrayed as holding to a rigid and one-dimensional line. For example, in a publication in this Series, Cecchin, Lane, and Ray (1992) state: "The feminist position conceptualizes violence towards women as being a product of women being victims of an oppressive male-dominated society." We wonder what constrains these authors—who are writing about irreverence—to be so reverent towards their own view of feminism.

Perhaps by stereotyping feminism as one fixed belief, its challenges and questions can be more easily ignored.

Systemic thinking has also been stereotyped in feminist writing, as when Deborah Luepnitz (1988) writes: "Explanations that begin with cybernetic presuppositions concentrate on how parts of the structure affect one another in a particular moment. They all emphasize in various ways that power is a myth and that the study of history is not of the utmost importance."

Reflecting on the development of our own thinking has triggered ideas about the processes by which dominant narratives of family therapy have been challenged by feminism. We have come to understand how the tension between taking fixed positions and having respect for multiple perspectives is itself a dialectic process. The process seems to go something like this:

1. We come to see that seemingly diverse ways of viewing the family and different models of therapy are in fact unitary—i.e. they all uncritically reflect the value system of a patriarchal society.
2. In order to justify making this critique, an alternative view (i.e. women are disempowered, blamed, and oppressed) is put forward which eschews complexity. This becomes "*the* feminist critique".
3. However, as this unitary view is maintained over time, there will eventually be more than one idea about what that view should be. One effect of these differences is fragmentation, discord, and less challenge to dominant narratives, as the argument rages about which unitary view represents the truth.
4. One way to avoid this is to accept a multiplicity of views and build on them as a strength; we can then talk of feminisms rather than feminism.[1]

Although we present this process as it occurs over time, it is also contextual. In certain contexts (i.e. in a conversation with someone representing an ultra-conservative view of families), we would feel impelled to present a coherent unitary view; in other contexts we feel much freer to explore contradictions.

Being aware of context enables us to accept that there will (hopefully) always be contradictions in our thinking. Sometimes we will be so organized by our anger about violence towards women that we feel like taking a radical separatist stance vis-à-vis men. At other times, we are more organized by the ways in which we, through our class, our race, our profession, participate in structures that are oppressive towards some men and other women. We thus consider it to be important that we do not always put gender as the highest order of context, but rather that we think about the question: "Highest order in which context?"

Knowing that we inevitably take different stances in different contexts gives us room to manouevre and keeps us free from the potentially mind-rotting state of "political correctness". (At the same time, however, we know that this label can be a convenient way for those uncomfortable about feminism to disqualify or ridicule its challenges.) This happens most powerfully when the process of challenging gender bias makes us aware of the constraints we then impose on our own thinking. So, for example, there was a time in our clinical work when we were so concerned about "mother blaming" in our society and in family therapy that we found ourselves working in opposition to this, tempted to frame all things women did as positive. This meant that we often missed important ambiguities and complexities in the work. It has been useful to keep asking ourselves questions such as: "What are we not allowing ourselves to see at the moment?" "What values would we least like to have challenged in this situation?"[2]

To give another example, our knowledge of how thoroughly women's experiences of sexual abuse have been denied or disqualified by professionals in the past has now made the question of whether some women could knowingly invent such stories virtually a taboo.

In adopting a feminist perspective throughout this book, we do not define feminist narrowly in the sense of only being concerned with issues for women, but as involving a critique of patriarchal social systems and the way they impact upon gendered experience at every level. This includes the constraints for men, too, of such a system of social organization. Feminism has proved to be a liberating as well as a challenging viewpoint for men. It has provided men with a context in which to think of their experience as gendered rather than as simply part of the natural order of things. As Stephen

Frosh (personal communication) has pointed out, feminism has made it possible for men, too, to think of themselves as "other".

We consider that gender, although based on biological difference, is socially constructed and that gendered meanings are open to challenge or confirmation. Throughout the book, we hold as a central theme the tension between, on the one hand, identifying and working with differences in men's and women's experiences at the societal, interpersonal, and intrapsychic levels, and, on the other, continually questioning these differences, because problems arise if and when such differences come to be seen as fixed and given. It is here that we think systemic thinking has so much to offer, because it provides an intellectually coherent way to expound contradictions and ambiguities.

We consider therapy to be a context in which people not only come for help with a specific problem, but also seek validation as people. Since we are all gendered persons, our clients' and our own gendered experiences, beliefs, and identities will either be validated or challenged in the process. However, although this may be generally accepted, for some therapists there will remain crucial and perhaps irreconcilable differences between feminist and systemic frameworks. Our view is that these differences are more to do with the context and beliefs of those who have developed and use the theories than with the inevitable qualities of the theories themselves.

One core belief for systemic thinkers is that ideas are co-created and do not exist in a vacuum, and Bateson (1972), par excellence, insisted on the need to overcome rigid boundaries between academic disciplines. Nevertheless, we cannot but be struck by the acontextual ways in which systemic ideas have been presented. The language and context of the ideas that have informed systemic therapists have inevitably been that of patriarchy, and therefore the way in which systemic thinking has been described and operationalized in therapy has been moulded by this context. This factor has led to an obscuring of those fundamentals of the systems approach which are consistent with the core, as we see it, of feminist thinking. What a systemic training has brought to our feminist thinking is an interactional understanding, including an understanding of belief systems, an appreciation of context and level, and a sensitivity to dilemmas of change for women and men in society.

As therapists we were initially very influenced by the approaches to dilemmas of change adopted by Peggy Papp and Olga Silverstein (Papp, 1983) and by Milan systemic therapy (Boscolo, Cecchin, Hoffman, & Penn, 1987). Latterly we work with a post-Milan narrative approach, strongly influenced by a social constructionist perspective. This means that we pay particular attention to language and narrative, to the way family and individual beliefs and meanings have evolved over time and how these have been influenced by societal beliefs.

When we address gender in therapy we try to hold in mind three levels. These are (1) the subjective level of gendered premises for individual men and women, (2) the way these premises are brought forth in interaction, i.e. the relational level, and (3) the societal constraints and opportunities for women and men and their impact on relationships and individual experience.

* * *

We have ordered the book so that each chapter either links theory and practice or is connected to another that moves its theme forward into the domain of therapy; case illustrations from our work are given throughout. We have put a major emphasis on theoretical discussions from feminist and systemic sources, because we think that an overview of the positive connections between feminism and systemic thinking is long overdue.

Chapter 1 outlines the ways in which we have thought about gender and how a feminist conceptualization of gender opens up a space for the constraints on both men and women to be addressed.

In Chapter 2, we explore constructivism, post-modernism, and social constructionism and their usefulness to feminist practice as well as some of the contradictions that emerge from them. The question of subjectivity, which provides the focus for Chapter 3, looks at concepts of self in our culture (linking individual experience and societal context), takes social constructionist ideas further, and develops a framework for understanding selfhood through gendered experience.

Chapter 4 returns to the key debate over power, still often viewed as a debate between two men (Bateson and Haley) and not always developed very fruitfully since. We return to Bateson for another conversation, but draw upon feminist voices that have contributed to this important debate but have often been ignored or stereotyped as "the feminist critique".

The next chapter, Chapter 5, follows up this theoretical argument with a presentation of our approach to work with physical and sexual violence and the particular dilemmas that working with such abuses of power involve for feminist and systemic therapists.

In Chapter 6, we describe narrative approaches to systemic therapy which, being based on recovering lost stories and lost knowledge, connect with feminist thinking and can validate and empower women's experience in particular.

In Chapter 7, we provide longer descriptions of our clinical work, including sections of transcripts that illustrate in more depth some of the ways in which we apply our thinking.

Chapters 8 and 9 raise issues for training and supervision and describe some training exercises that we have found helpful in stimulating thinking about gender issues. Chapter 10 forms the conclusion of the book.

Throughout the book, we have aimed to explore and sustain contradictions rather than to overcome them. This may be a truism of the systemic approach, but it is equally a statement about our own understanding of what is best about feminist thinking—when it embraces contradictions and finds ambiguity a stimulus to further thought rather than a state to be rationalized, closed down, or avoided.

Notes

1. It can be argued that the history of socialism shows how, in the context of much left-wing politics, this evolution never really took place. No single faction was ever ready to give up its claim to unitary truth for the sake of the movement as a whole.

2. Similar questions in a different context were posed by Glenda Fredman (1990), many of which we have adapted specifically to gender.

CHAPTER 1

Gender:
a systemic understanding

This book addresses how our preoccupations with gender interweave with our systemic thinking and practice, and so we begin by examining gender.

We use the word gender, as different from biological sex which is assigned from birth on the basis of genital difference, to mean the way societies think about and live that sexual difference. Until the last few decades, gender difference was, on the whole, seen as equivalent to sex difference—real, natural, and fixed. However, feminists have brought into question many of the previously held "common-sense" ideas of what it means to be men and women in our society. They have challenged many of the givens of gender and uncovered ways in which our society constructs the concepts of female and male, while at the same time this construction remains hidden.

This argument that "femininity" and "masculinity" are social constructions, built on biological difference but given significance by and through the power relationships in our society, is a central tenet of our thinking. The main tension in this position lies in the way our world has been divided along gender lines, so that, although our gender is mere construction, we tend to experience it as absolute and central to our subjectivity. Grappling with these inherent contradictions has raised interesting and, we think, crucial questions both theoretically and in our clinical work.

Our society explicitly states that it wishes to foster gender equality, but at the same time it continues to preserve structures of domination (Benjamin, 1990). This contributes to many paradoxical experiences. It is particularly difficult to hold on to these contradictions when a satisfactory relationship between a woman and a man exists in which both partners believe in equality, and yet in many contexts they remain unequal. Many of us veer from minimizing to exaggerating gender difference depending on the circumstances; but neither stance moves us to a new paradigm with which to think about gender. It is here that a systemic framework offers a way to think about the individual, relational, and societal levels at which we experience gender and to explore contradictions between them.

THE CONTEXT OF PATRIARCHY

For systemic thinkers, understanding context is crucial, and in the case of gender this includes the wider societal context. The context of patriarchy renders the meaning of gender difference inseparable from the experience of inequality; in turn, societal structures and social practices—including language, the law, education, etc.—both reflect and produce this meaning. Identifying these connections enables other ideas and meanings about gender to emerge, as well as bringing into question the inevitability of societies based on what Eisler (1987) has termed a dominator model.

We consider it essential to believe in the reality (although not the inevitability) of patriarchy. We make this point because views that propose that there is no such thing as reality, but only whatever an observer "chooses" to see, have recently become fashionable (see Chapter 2). These views label feminists as "choosing" to see sexist interactions and conveniently dismiss or even blame them for constructing the problem themselves.

THEORIES OF GENDER

Understanding gender is a complicated task because our gender so profoundly shapes our identities and experiences. Because gender works as an organizing mode of perception and belief which underlies much of what we talk about as well as how we live our lives, it has been a difficult task to isolate specific influences as gendered. A systemic view helps us clarify the confusion of levels that results from trying to observe something to which you cannot be "meta" (Goldner et al., 1990).

A systemic framework has not yet been applied to an analysis of gendered identities. In the systemic field there has been more of a preoccupation with therapy and change than with understanding human development as such. Feminist family therapists have therefore tended to draw on feminist psychoanalytic work (such as Benjamin, 1990; Chodorow, 1978; Dinnerstein, 1976; Luepnitz, 1988) to provide more radical interpretations of individual gendered experience.

What is femaleness and maleness? The question implies that somewhere, somehow, we could really find out what womanhood and manhood is. We take the view that these categories have been created through language, which in turn has real effects on how we live, think, and feel. This is not to deny that there are actual biological differences, but that these are so profoundly mediated through culture that it is impossible to find a gendered essence; we can only discover the ways in which we "perform" these differences.

So, for example, there are considerable differences in the ways parents behave from the moment that they discover whether their baby is a girl or a boy. When it is difficult to assign a biological sex to a baby because of organic anomalies, there is enormous discomfort because a genderless baby seems too much of a challenge to our beliefs. Parents' and other caretakers' interactions with a baby are shaped by their culture's beliefs about babies and in particular their gender. One study found that within 24 hours of birth, daughters were already described differently from sons (smaller, softer, etc.) although there were no differences in size and weight (Rubin, Provenzano, & Luria, 1974). Parents draw on prevalent gender beliefs to develop a narrative about and with their babies, which then shapes the interactional patterns that develop. When they cried, boys were believed to be angry and frustrated, whereas girls were seen to be sad and depressed (Maccoby & Jacklin, 1974). Other studies found that mothers generally held boys more than girls, talked more to girls, and weaned girls earlier than boys (Olivier, 1989). Unfortunately, some research into how infants acquire a sense of self through narratives developed in their relationships (Stern, 1985) has neglected to mention gender at all!

In therapy we often ask questions that tap the family's gendered narratives. Questions to children along the lines of "What if you were a girl and your sister was a boy?" produce fascinating responses and open up areas for parents and children that have clearly never been thought about before.

The theoretical work that has grappled with the question of how gender identities are formed has ranged from ideas about sex-role assignment to psychoanalytic theory. Although some of these theoretical concepts helpfully describe gender, they also mainly reflect the ways in which gender difference is embedded in our society. Sex-role theorists like Bem (1973), for example, ended up contributing to rather fixed ideas about female and male characteristics. After examining the psychoanalytic literature, Benjamin (1990) argued that much of this writing simply reproduces the polarizations of gender differences rather than questions them. For example, she demonstrated the way psychoanalysis continually constructed mothers as people without subjectivity of their own or as feared archaic figures, while fathers stand for progress and reality. This theorizing illustrates the dangers of ignoring the context of our theory building.

Feminist theorists' efforts to understand gendered arrangements can also be seen to contribute to them. Feminist object relation theorist Chodorow (1978) is a good example of this. She reworked traditional psychoanalytic formulations about gender identity to argue that mothers were of central importance in reproducing traditional and problematized gendered identities. Girls' identities, she argued, were constructed through mutual identification with their devalued mothers, characterized by boundary confusions and sensitivity to others' needs rather than their own. Boys' identities were based on differentiation from their mothers, which conveyed value and agency on them but was predicated on staying distant and separate from femaleness. Chodorow saw childcare arrangements as maintaining these troublesome gendered identities and relationships, and she believed these would change only if childcare was shared equally by both parents. Chodorow broke new ground by exploring the development of girls as well as boys and by keeping the societal context and its meanings central, but she and others who have used her work have been criticized by other feminists for shoring up essentializing views of gender and mothering. (By essentializing we mean the belief that there is an "essence" of gender which can be identified.) Systemic thinking, with its emphasis on the relationship between relationships, introduces a more fluid and contextual view (see Goldner's paper, "Toward a Critical Relational Theory of Gender", 1991, for an attempt to synthesize systemic concepts with psychoanalytic theory).

Historical, psychoanalytic, and anthropological studies can really only provide hypotheses about how gendered differences are "produced" through our relationships and cultural practices, and why our gender has been so central to the way we experience ourselves. An irreverent stance (Cecchin et al., 1992) to these hypotheses helps us generate pertinent questions about their context.

WHY HAS GENDER DIFFERENCE BEEN SO IMPORTANT?

One of the most striking aspects of gender in all societies is how important it has been to emphasize and promote gender difference. Gender was constructed as a dualistic category: that is, male and female were thought of as opposite and polarized—female cannot be male, masculine is what is not feminine. Traditional gender characteristics were fixed at opposite ends of continuums (such as active–passive, instrumental–nurturing, rational–emotional) and seen to be natural and inherent properties of men and women. Butler (1990) argued that these gender polarities were centrally linked to the idea of the inevitability and necessity of heterosexuality.

However, gender roles were not always so fixed and polarized. Keller (1985) in her study of the origins of modern science, described the multiplicity of male and female roles offering heterogeneity that were available before the seventeenth century. These were considerably reduced when the rise of early industrial capitalism led to a separation of life into public and private domains, with increasingly limited and polarized roles. Rationality associated with maleness became valued at the time that science was established as a discipline, while alchemists and witchcraft associated with the dangerousness and irrationality of women were dismissed (Chamberlain, 1981; Keller, 1985). Many of these polarizations have lasted until well into this century, although we may now be witnessing their breakdown.

THE PROCESS OF CHANGE

We live in a time when these gendered polarizations have been brought into question. Feminists began to argue that to move away from gender stereotypes would be advantageous for women's mental health, because so many female characteristics were devalued by society as a whole. As this was taken up by women in the private as well as the public arena, men experienced this possible collapse of traditional gender differences as potentially disastrous. It started to become clear that the polarization of gender difference may have been more essential for males than females.

This could be understood in the light of ideas developed by those feminist writers who had argued that masculine identity was formed through a process of disidentifying with the mother/woman and refuting anything female (Chodorow, 1978; Dinnerstein, 1976; Mead, 1950). In our society, masculinity has been profoundly tied to its distance from (and therefore dependence on) femininity; men needed to stay at a distance from anything associated with women and to retain control—of themselves, of women, and of nature (Frosh, 1994). Because this was a never-ending process, it has been argued that a sense of masculinity is never secure (Mead, 1950; Segal, 1990) (see also Chapter 5). We think that this continual need to reaffirm maleness, and the power associated with it, has limited the possibilities for men to challenge gendered arrangements in the ways that have proved so liberating for numbers of women, and has also contributed to the feelings of panic and confusion described by men who struggled to adapt to feminism (Norton, 1991; Seidler, 1991).

RELATIONAL DILEMMAS OF CHANGE

With a systemic framework, it has been possible to explore the gender premises that influence women and men in relationships and the dilemmas involved in change. Gender characteristics and premises can be seen as interactional and relational, not belonging to individual women and men but to the relationships between them as they have developed over time. We can also question how far these qualities characterize relationships of inequality, rather than gender as such.

Case example
"I'll take care of the worry"

A woman referred herself for some help because she was depressed, and the therapist decided to ask the couple to come to the session. The woman presented herself as crippled by anxiety, often tearful, and worried that she might be damaging her children. Her husband saw her depression as the problem and wanted to know what he could do to help her with managing things better. The couple described how they had recently set up a business but this was now on the brink of failing because of the recession. He stayed optimistic and cheerful in the face of great financial worries, although he was concerned about the effects on his wife and children. The wife's anxiety could be seen to be allowing her husband to demonstrate optimism, which was necessary in their advertising business where a positive outlook was essential. His cheerfulness, on the other hand, meant that she felt she had to worry more about the realities of the possibility of failure. As a therapy team we became interested in what could not be said and which experiences could not be described. The therapist then asked the couple what would have happened if the wife had been in charge of the business. This allowed another description of experience to emerge in which this woman was torn between feeling she had to support her husband's business decisions as a wife, and her own ideas about what would be useful. And her husband went on to talk about the strains of having to be a superman.

Research has shown how the most stereotypical gender behaviour is brought forth in the context of male–female relationships (Skrypnek & Snyder, 1982). When people were blindly paired with a partner, they reacted very differently depending on whether they believed they were paired with someone of the same or the opposite gender. This research fits with our clinical experience of working with families who have separated and divorced, where both women and men found they developed different qualities once they were parenting and living on their own (see Burck & Daniel, 1994, for a fuller discussion).

We see men's and women's relationships with each other as saturated with premises about gender, embedded in and demonstrated over and over again in family and community relationships, as well as explicitly stated in sayings or stories. Each individual is thus not only connected to premises infused from a past network of relationships, but to the interlocking premises, beliefs, and behaviours of the partner. This becomes even more complex when we examine some of the more common gender premises in our society, and how these are played out. Individuals and families often report being influenced by contradictory messages, or messages that were in contradiction with the community as a whole. One example is that of gendered messages about strength and weakness, in which a belief that men were strong and capable and women fragile and needing to be looked after existed alongside a belief that men were actually fragile and needed to be protected by emotionally strong and enduring women. As these beliefs often operate in different contexts, the contradictions may not prove too disruptive, and yet they are difficult to challenge because they are immediately counteracted by the other belief, leaving a sense of a tightly constrained and paradoxical system. Although this may be a feature of many relationships, it is in heterosexual relationships that it seems most fixed.

In recent years, most of the pressure for personal, familial, and societal change has come from women. This has faced women with a number of dilemmas, as these struggles have often occurred in the context of intimate loving relationships with men on whom they depend and through whom they may define their sense of self (Daniel, 1986). Women may blame their male partners for lack of change, with little realization of how powerfully their own gender premises may restrict their choices and also sensitize them to their partners' requests to continue with old ways within the new forms. Similarly, men may attempt to become non-dominant, only to use this as a way of keeping control of their relationships (see Norton, 1991, for an interesting discussion of how "new men" manage this in their sexual relationships). Moving to new experiences in gendered relationships involves struggling with ourselves as well as the beliefs and actions of our partners and communities.

Case example
"My daughter won't let me live my life"
A mother and adult daughter who lived together came to therapy because of the daughter's depression. The father had died three years earlier, and the daughter, an only child, had been very close to him. The mother had developed a relationship with another man, and the daughter appeared very resentful of this. After some sessions of therapy, the daughter became much less depressed, took a job, and started to go out more. However, conflict between mother and daughter escalated, with the mother complaining bitterly about the daughter's selfishness and that she was not "allowing" her to have the same freedom that she (the daughter) now had. When the mother was asked how she would now like to live her life, she could only respond by criticizing her daughter. This pattern only shifted when the therapist explored the mother's life history, which had been entirely constructed around giving up her own needs for others and acknowledged how terrifying this present stage must be for her. Within this frame, the daughter could be seen as helping her mother by giving her the opportunity to fight for her own self-development.

We think there is much to be learned by exploring the different meanings given to gender in different cultural and social contexts, and through these variations to loosen gender constraints and question gendered knowledge. The different gendered experiences of people living in less-traditional family forms, like single-parent households or gay/lesbian relationships, are useful because, although they carry the potential for replicating traditional patterns, they can also be contexts in which gendered realities can be transformed (Giddens, 1992). Race, culture, and class all help us think about the possibilities and variations in different contexts. In Denmark, for example, where there is an equal gender mix in parliament and the state provides child care to enable women and men to enter the working world more equitably, women and men have developed less polarized relationships (Blow, personal communication). Gjuricova (1992), on the other hand, has discussed how difficult it was even to reflect on gender difference in Czechoslovakia, because there is no word for "gender" in their vocabulary.

Despite differences in race and cultural background, many people we have worked with have identified very similar beliefs about women and men, although there have been considerable variations in how these beliefs were lived. A woman of Caribbean origin, for example, was astonished to find beliefs about the peripheralness of fathers held in the families and communities of some of her white British and Irish colleagues, as this is often considered characteristic of Caribbean families. Beliefs identified by British families about women holding responsibility for men's sexuality is embedded in the legal system in judgments about women's implication in rape. In Muslim countries and communities, it is especially women who have the responsibility not to tempt the men by displaying themselves (Lau, 1994). What has been useful to discover is that many people who have been trying to change their behaviour and relationships are still profoundly influenced by beliefs about gender of which they were not really aware. We have learned that maintaining curiosity about these beliefs has changed individuals' and families' relationships to them, allowing alternatives to emerge.

THERAPEUTIC DILEMMAS ABOUT GENDER

Many therapists are unclear about when and how to think about gender in their work. Some clinicians have argued that therapists have no right to introduce ideas about gender, as this would be political and is not what clients have come to therapy for. Others say it is immoral not to think about gender, as otherwise one is condoning and supporting arrangements that seriously disadvantage women and are also restricting for men.

Although in our experience few people come for help specifically with a problem that they have defined in terms of gender, much (if not all) our clinical thinking encompasses ideas about gender constructions. At times, these form the background to other preoccupations; at other times, it is useful to bring them to the forefront in order to highlight premises that might be organizing lives and relationships. Families and individuals are then better able to know which they would like to alter.

In therapeutic work, we are individuals working with individual women and men, girls and boys. Gender sensitivity in the work can prove liberating but can also hold dangers. Problems experienced as personal and pathological can be helpfully reframed as connected to social and societal constraints, and feminist-inspired therapy can thus make individual men feel less, rather than more, blamed. However, therapists who invite women to buy the idea that the relationship between them and their partners can be changed solely by making the right choices, ignoring wider social and structural constraints (hooks, 1989, 1991), may exacerbate stress by conveying a sense of blame if these changes do not happen!

We believe that the ways in which "femininity" and "masculinity" have been constructed and lived in our society are problematic for both women and men and operate as unhelpful constraints on individuals trying to live and sort out their difficulties together. As Goldner (1991b) argued:

> . . . the exploitation of gender distinctions in the inevitable struggle for power in society and domestic life produces untenable relationship binds and unbridgeable psychic splits, which damage the human spirit in all of us and in the next generation. [p. 271]

As therapists, we cannot *not* take gender into account when meeting with families, the question is much more *how* we do it. Creating a liveable "mixed marriage" (Jones, 1990) between feminist ideologies and systemic paradigms requires a reexamination of their potential for compatibility, and we now explore this in Chapter 2.

CHAPTER 2

Feminisms and other "isms"

> "The power of patriarchy has been extremely difficult to understand because it is all-pervasive. It has influenced our most basic ideas about human nature and about our relation to the universe—'man's' nature and 'his' relation to the universe, in patriarchal language. It is the one system which, until recently, had never in recorded history been openly challenged, and whose doctrines were so universally accepted that they seemed to be laws of nature."
>
> Fritjof Capra (1982, p. 29)

> "As a result of what has been, quite literally, 'the study of man', most social scientists have had to work with such an incomplete and distorted data base that in any other context it would immediately have been recognised as deeply flawed."
>
> Riane Eisler (1987, p. xviii)

When we think about the development of feminist ideas and critiques, we are reminded of what Bateson (1972) wrote about levels of learning. He defined three different levels of learning, which he related to our understanding of the context in which we learn. The extent to which we understand context determines the kinds of questions we ask or do not ask, and therefore what we know or do not know.

Learning at Level I is similar to behavioural or rote learning in which the same stimulus triggers similar responses; this is learning in the way Pavlov's dogs learnt to salivate at the sound of a bell. Level II involves learning about the context and acting according to an understanding of the rules and premises of the context in which learning takes place. Bateson argues that Learning II acquired in early life is likely to persist throughout life, because of the self-validating nature of the behaviour that ensues. Learning at Level III, Bateson says, is difficult and rare, even in human beings. It involves facing the contradictions between premises, and questioning the context of the context of learning in which the rules we live by are embedded; this involves a profound redefinition of the self and an attempt to resolve contrary premises, which, Bateson argues, can often lead to the label of craziness.

Something akin to Bateson's idea of learning at Level III has been involved in feminist challenges to patriarchal patterns of thought, and it is, therefore, no coincidence that women who did challenge these premises were in the past described and treated as if they were mad.

An example of the constraining and confusing binds placed on women who sought "unacceptable" roles for themselves is given by Henry Maudesley:

> In this matter, the small minority of women who have other aims and pant for other careers, cannot be accepted as the spokeswomen of their sex.... If they are right, they will have deserved well the success which will reward their faith and works; if they are wrong, the error will avenge itself upon them and their children, if they should ever have any. In the worst, even they will

not have been without their use as failures; for they will have furnished experiments to aid us in arriving at correct judgements concerning the capacities of women and their right functions in the universe. [quoted in Showalter, 1987]

Feminist thinkers who challenge established academic disciplines still often feel that their success or failure will reflect not only on themselves, but also on all women. (Perhaps now, however, feelings of craziness are less likely to come from questioning the unquestionable than from trying to make sense of the massive amount of literature that has been spawned in the wake of such questioning and from trying to unravel the different theories that have accompanied it!)

DEFINITIONS

Much feminist scholarship has influenced and been influenced by the intellectually fashionable theories that have recently been taken up by family therapists. These include "Constructivism", "Post-Modernism", "Deconstruction", and "Social Constructionism", terms that have been used liberally in recent family therapy literature, often without sufficient definition. Here we clarify their differences before discussing their advantages and disadvantages for feminist thinkers and practitioners.

The terms constructivism and post-modernism are sometimes used as if they were interchangeable, and they do indeed share a common intellectual heritage, which includes Kant and the idealist philosophers Hegel and Nietzsche. This tradition of thought does not make a distinction between ontology (the study of the object world) and epistemology (the theory of knowledge); in other words, *what* we know is inseparable from *how* we know it. There can thus be no objective description of reality; the theory that we bring to such a description determines the nature of what we see. However, the constructivist theories that first influenced family therapists stemmed from the field of biology, and in particular the **radical constructivist** work of Maturana (1970, 1988, 1991), Maturana and Varela (1980), and von Glaserfeld (1991). Their ideas share the common premise that what we call "reality" is a product of the "perceptual and conceptual structures which we manage to establish, use and maintain in the flow of our actual experience" (von Glaserfeld, 1991). Cognition and perception are therefore prime objects of study.

Post-modernism, by contrast, has evolved primarily in a European context of literary and intellectual criticism and has been concerned with analysing the limitations of Western scholarship, in particular its claims to universalizing theories. It has been described as representing "incredulity towards metanarratives" (Lyotard 1989), by which is meant those narratives which come to represent social or intellectual norms. Instead, all narratives are seen by post-modernists as being legitimate simply by virtue of their being lived and told (Frosh, 1991) (see also Chapter 4, where we explore this theme further).

Deconstruction is the analytic tool through which the post-modernist process of undermining "grand narratives" takes place. It involves a method of interpretation based on the tension between what is said and what is not said within texts, traditions, or discourses (Derrida, 1967). Interpretation based on deconstruction attempts to make visible what is absent through undermining the philosophies on which these discourses are based. An example of this is how feminist critics exposed the gendered assumptions that lie behind many family therapy approaches and showed how these are revealed through language—for example, that of strategic therapy (Burck & Daniel, 1990; Hoffman, 1985) or structural therapy where men's and women's power in families has been connoted differently by therapists (Walters, 1990). The common thread is the undermining of those systems of thought that claim objectivity or universality.

Another body of theory with a long tradition in sociology and social psychology (Berger & Luckman, 1966; Gergen, 1985; Giddens, 1992; Shotter, 1993) which has recently been very influential among family therapists is that of **social constructionism**. This differs from constructivism in that it places the emphasis, not on the the cognitive processing of the observer, but on the language in which this processing takes place. Thus accounts of the world, in science and elsewhere, are not viewed as

> . . . the external expression of the speaker's internal processes (such as cognition, intention) but as an expression of relation-

ships between persons. From this viewpoint, it is within social interaction that language is generated, sustained and abandoned. ... The analysis draws attention to the manner in which conventions of language and other social processes influence the accounts rendered of the "objective" world. The emphasis is thus not on the individual mind but on the meanings generated by people as they collectively generate descriptions and explanations in language. [Gergen, 1991]

THE FEMINIST PROJECT

These "isms" have provided useful critical tools for feminist thinkers to highlight the value base of many different disciplines, including therapy. Much feminist research has been carried out to further this process and has involved the recovery of female achievements in the arts, literature, and politics (e.g. Kaplan, 1986; Ncobo, 1988; Spender, 1982; Warner, 1985). A particularly powerful example of challenging a supposedly objective body of knowledge has been the work of Evelyn Keller (1985). She argues that our image of science as an emotionally and sexually neutral abstract body of theory is itself a cultural myth. She demonstrates how, from the days of Francis Bacon and the birth of the scientific method, down to the present, science has been consistently depicted as a masculine force mastering a female nature (Goldner, 1985). In psychology, two writers who have had a major impact by challenging the hegemony of male-biased theories are Jean Baker Miller (1976) and Carol Gilligan (1982); they have both advanced alternative accounts of emotional development, based on the different socialization processes that women experience. Miller develops her critique of conventional theories of female psychology by exploring the meaning of female/male interaction in the context of dominant–subordinant relationships. In particular she looks at the way "de-selfing" is culturally prescribed for women. This stereotyped behaviour then becomes labelled as a personality trait, which is in turn taken as evidence of female psychology. By analysing the context of power in female/male relationships, Miller "unpacks" the paradox of stereotyped behaviour in women being simultaneously classed as pathology (Broverman et al., 1970) and as cultural prescription.

In a sense, all of these feminist writers are engaged in a process of "deconstruction". As they critique academic disciplines and reveal the gendered beliefs and assumptions that lie behind supposedly "objective" analyses of data, they challenge the idea of unitary truth and highlight the absence of the female voice.

However, the relationship between feminism and these other "isms" also contains some contradictions and dilemmas for feminist thinkers and practitioners. Firstly, how far do theories that focus on the way we construct reality, rather than on reality itself, actually challenge the intellectual status quo? How much, by polarizing subject and object, are they just repeating age-old gendered patterns of thought in a different form? Secondly, how much can theories that aim specifically to undermine ideologies be used to challenge oppression? Do they not also undermine alternative ideologies and any coherent programmes for action that might stem from them? Both these questions lead us to restate a core question for systemic thinkers: "What is it that is changing in order that something else does not have to change?"

CONSTRUCTIVISM

One of the ways in which the ideas of the radical constructivists—Maturana, von Glaserfeld, and Von Foerster—have been most useful to family therapists is in their scepticism about the concept of truth. When families, or families and professionals, are engaged in battles over "truth", a constructivist frame that incorporates many different truths is invaluable. Professionals are most at risk of being abusive to families and individuals when they are convinced that they know the truth.

Claims to objective truth always involve a denial of the way others see the world because they define those views as false or partial. Therapists who talk about their clients "lacking insight" are falling into just this trap. Seeing truth as proven by evidence from the real world also absolves the observer from the responsibility of specifying his or her ways of knowing that truth. As Maturana (1991) says, the belief in the ownership of truth leads directly to the "blind alley of fanaticism", and linked with this "ownership" of truth comes the danger of abandoning responsibility for one's own actions because they can be justified as being in the service of that truth. Responsibility can thus only come from reflection on our own actions and on the thinking that led to them. The use of observing teams in therapy provides such a framework for questioning the therapist's construction of reality.

A focus on how we know what we know is of obvious relevance to the question of gender, because we can use constructivist ideas to question the observer-dependent nature of so-called truths about human development, which claim to be "objective" but in fact reflect one gendered view. So, for example, much of Piaget's work on cognitive development was based on assumptions about development which actually put boys' development as of a higher order than that of girls. As Gilligan (1982) demonstrated in her analysis of Kohlberg's work on moral development, assumptions about what constitutes the highest stage of development are not challenged in the light of the research findings that women are less likely to reach this stage than men.

However, what Gilligan's work also demonstrates is the danger that, in putting forward an alternative theory of women's development, this in turn can become equally fixed and unchallenged. We are faced with the paradox that we cannot demonstrate what is missing without defining the "something" that is left out; but in defining this, we run the risk of an alternative view of reality that may become equally limited, unitary, and static.

If we take a constructivist frame to avoid this trap, it leads us into a primary focus on our own knowing rather than on what we observe. This can be very useful in querying statements about gender and questioning our own assumptions. One of us [GD] was looking at a videotape of work with a couple where she was questioning the husband about some generalized statements he made about women, which he used to explain his wife's behaviour. Following questions about how he had come to this knowledge about women, the husband eventually said: "I suppose I'm a bit of a male chauvinist pig, really." She was shocked to see herself nodding sagely at this revelation, as if she and he had finally arrived at some truth, rather than continuing to explore what he meant by this!

We think, however, that there are difficulties in the way that constructivism promotes the idea of subject-centred reason. The problem with a primary focus on cognition is that it presupposes a separation between subject and object. This leads to more of an engagement with ways of knowing rather than with our relationship to that which we know. Jessica Benjamin (1990) has described this arbitary separation of subject and object as "the transcendental subject" eating up "the reality of the world". She challenges the idea that it is necessary to give up the scientific project of knowing the world and to substitute for it the belief that everything in the world is in the eye of the beholder, because this process leads to "sucking the life out of the social and natural world" (Benjamin, 1990).

Taking this theme further, if we think about our world as traditionally constructed with a "male subject" and "female or feminized object", this can be seen as a means of continuing to emphasize masculine agency at the expense of understanding that "feminized" world differently.

Here, it is useful to put the development of these ideas in context. Constructivist ideas from the 1970s onwards evolved during a time in which the impossibility of controlling the natural world and its resources was increasingly recognized. How in this context is a sense of agency maintained? By shifting the focus from the nature of the "objective world" to an exploration of how we know what we know of the world, we are bound to think differently about making the world subject to our control. One direction in which radical constructivism could be seen to lead is an effective dismissal of the nature of the physical world. The point is illustrated by physicist Dana Zohar (1990), who says that a popular misapprehension arising from the oft-quoted finding that, depending on the instrument, electrons can be seen as particle or wave, is to draw the conclusion that what is seen is in the eye of the beholder. In fact, she argues, the choice is only between particle and wave, so what we see is also determined by the reality of the physical world, rather than solely by our own cognitive structures.

We would argue, therefore, that the "retreat into subjectivity" can be seen as a reassertion of agency, one that perpetuates a split between subject and object at the expense of understanding the relationship between them. A second critique of this denial of the objective nature of the world is that it makes it difficult intellectually to justify a political position. Colapinto (1985) criticizes Maturana's apoliticism in the following terms:

> We can focus on being ourselves, look inward for coherent meanings, live in the serene equanimity of our own customized

bubbles. We can take flight from external chaos into inner stability, Walkmanise our existence and still feel epistemologically justified. [p. 30]

Maturana—understandably, perhaps, in the political context of Pinochet's Chile—appears to be hostile to the idea of adopting or holding to any ideology. For feminists, the logical conclusion of constructivist thinking would be that the central tenet of *its* ideology—i.e. the existence of patriarchy—can have no external validity but is no more than a construction in the mind of those who believe it. It is just one truth among many.

Thus, while radical constructivism provides a helpful stance to understand our own thinking as well as that of others, it has limitations for taking a moral stance on issues of oppression or abuses of power (see Chapters 4 and 5 for further discussion). Its emphasis on subject-centred reality can also detract from, rather than enhance, the process of making connections and thus taking collective action. In addition, the emphasis on subject-centred reality implicit in constructivism also has its parallels in a kind of feminism that emphasizes the uniqueness of women's experience, focuses on an exploration of women's subjectivity, and promotes what Virginia Goldner (1991a) refers to as the "dogmatism of the intuitive". This reduction of women's experience both denies women's capacity to "use logic and theory as tools of knowing" (Goldner, 1991a) and ignores other contexts such as race or class which impact on and shape women's lives.

POST-MODERNISM

Post-modernism does provide us with a framework within which to address differences and challenge polarities. The post-modernist stance enables us to talk of feminisms, a "patchwork of overlapping alliances, not one circumscribable by an essential definition" (Nicholson, 1990). Differences between women are seen to be as important as what unites them. This enables us to value difference between women in terms of class, race, or sexuality rather than obscuring such differences under the category of gender.

A post-modernist account of the world seems to fit intuitively with most women's lived experience—i.e. of multiple and often conflicting allegiances to family, friends, household, and work, of holding on to worries about a sick child or vulnerable elderly parent whilst working at a busy supermarket checkout or addressing a conference. As we argue in the next chapter, traditional male constructions of self may make it more difficult for men to handle such multiple and contradictory experiences. However, while post-modernist ideas seem to reflect well the experiences of fragmentation and saturation that many individuals live in the modern world, this virtual celebration of fragmentation does pose dilemmas.

Much of the same criticism about constructivism's apolitical stance can also be levelled at post-modernism. Post-modernism can be seen to fit very well with an atomized, consumer society, where we are led to believe that ideology is a thing of the past, where the illusion of choice masks the unequal distribution of resources, and where truth is seen as primarily a matter of presentation. We find the metaphor of consumers revealing here, because while intellectually all narratives may be seen to be equally valid and access to print no longer the province of the elite, in our society, at any rate, this theoretical trend has been accompanied by a massive shift of resources from the poor to the rich. Consumers' satisfaction, at their access to a dazzling array of goods and services and a vast amount of information about their rights, tends to be blunted by the lack of means to pay for them. Thus we have to look with some scepticism at a theoretical stance that accords all narratives equal status but would also undermine any alternative "meta-narrative". Post-modernism (like the concept of therapeutic neutrality, which assumed that the therapist could give equal weight to all positions) is therefore implicated in ignoring context—i.e. our society, which neither confers equal validity and status to all views, nor provides the resources for all views to become established in practice.

Many feminists, and black feminists in particular (hooks, 1989, 1991), have described the irony that, just as radical black and feminist perspectives are emerging strongly to challenge the social order, a philosophical stance is being constructed that incorporates all views, without taking a position on the way our society should be ordered. It is in this context that we find most pertinent Luce Irigaray's (1985) question about whether post-modernism is the last ruse of patriarchy.

However, post-modernism as a framework for addressing differences and understanding fragmentation is important. Deconstruction is a critical tool that can and should be turned on feminist discourses themselves (Goldner, 1991a) particularly when "woman" and "woman's experience" have been presented as universal. Black women have been powerful and trenchant critics of white Western feminists who assume that their dilemmas represent core issues for all women. For example, those white middle-class women who focus on the power and privilege of white middle-class men may ignore the dilemmas of women who also have to address directly racial and class oppression and its impact on their men's lives as well as on their own.

SOCIAL CONSTRUCTIONISM

All theories that focus more on the subject's beliefs and experience than on the "objective" nature of the world pose dilemmas for those thinkers and practitioners who deal with the impact of oppression. As we have seen, constructivism and post-modernism both raise questions about how, if all views are only views, we can critique the processes whereby some views come to be accorded more status than others. The issue of power is clearly central here and is the subject of Chapter 4.

Social constructionism, because it focuses more on the interactive nature of our relationship to the object world, does offer us a means to understand how our experience is not just a product of our individual cognition, but socially constructed. It can help us understand the way that major social and economic changes shape our internal experiences (Giddens, 1992; Shotter, 1993). Shotter argues that realist and social constructionist standpoints are not incompatible, because "claims about the social constructions people *could* produce remain purely theoretical unless also accompanied by some kind of claims about the actual or real possibilities (and resources required) for such constructions to be available to them in their circumstances" (Shotter, 1993). This fits very well with our own therapeutic stance, which focuses on the contexts in which people could have their stories validated. Therapy may be the first such context (and for many psychoanalytic therapists, remains the primary one) for developing new stories, but for systemic therapists the question of what resources—relational or material—are available is a crucial one. For example, many women begin to experience themselves in a different way after divorce; but, "ironically, as women expand their stories of self, they also face the constraints and dilemmas associated with the pragmatics of single parenting, e.g. childcare responsibilities and financial problems. Poverty is hardly the most helpful context in which to develop new thinking and expand horizons" (Burck & Daniel, 1994).

Social constructionist stances, by concentrating on the language used to describe objective experiences, can help us understand how that language fixes and constrains us. An example of this is the problematic description of "single-parent families". The term "lone parent", often used in preference, carries with it a welter of meanings, including "only" and "lonely", each of which discounts the existence either of the other parent or of other important relationships like family or friends. The term "female-headed household" carries with it the assumption that two-parent families are "male-headed". Such descriptions have to be set in the context of dominant narratives about normal families (Burck & Daniel, 1994).

We find it particularly useful to ask people in therapy what sources they have relied on to determine what they know. Questioning how individuals have come to see themselves in the ways they do often reveals relational origins that lend new perspectives to these descriptions and open up alternatives.

Social constructionist approaches also provide a framework for thinking about history, for exploring the evolution of ideas over time and through language, thus challenging their fixed and immutable nature. On a recent visit to Pompeii, where we were shown the dining room with its adjacent vomitorium, we wondered whether bulimia could possibly have been seen as pathological in ancient Rome!

CONCLUSION

Just as the influence of feminism in all its forms has been fundamental in shaping what can be loosely summarized as the "new epistemology", which involves multiple ways of viewing the world, so the different philosophical stances this has given rise to have provided feminism with further useful critical tools.

Constructivism, post-modernism, and social constructionism have been helpful in reminding us that our feminist view is not the truth, nor the only feminist view, but a way to highlight some of the not-so-obvious beliefs and assumptions embedded in the way families and therapists make sense of their experiences. It helps us maintain a critical stance on some feminist writing that advocates the superiority of "women's ways". While we can expose ways in which knowledge has traditionally been produced, we need to be mindful not to fall into the trap of replicating stereotypes by maintaining dualistic ways of constructing knowledge.

Making explicit generalizations about gender is not to create truth but is a part of a process of unpacking and acknowledging gender difference. In this way we hope to maintain a curiosity about gender which raises questions about how men and women come to know themselves and their relationships and how this knowledge is affected by the societal context. Thinking about how our own constructions of gender are socially influenced most importantly helps us explore and be curious about the descriptions we use and how they vary from context to context.

CHAPTER 3

Gender and subjectivity

When we think about subjectivity, we usually think about unique, personal, and private experiences, without any awareness of how we have been influenced by societal beliefs about "the self". It is a mark of how powerfully our society is organized around the concept of individualism that most of us are loath to admit to this societal influence.

In this chapter we discuss some ideas about gender and subjectivity. The context of gender illuminates the constructions and constraints of our experiences of selfhood in a way that clarifies the impact of society on intimate relationships and subjective experience. These ideas have enabled us to bring societal connections into therapy at the most personal level.

We consider subjectivity to include both the experience of self—experiences that make up selfhood—and our reflections on this selfhood, all of which affect each other. We live the story of ourselves and describe it to ourselves and others in an on-going way. This self-narrative also encompasses our premises, thoughts, and feelings, which shape and are, in turn, shaped by our experiences. Interesting work in child development has attempted to detail and theorize the emergence of an infant's sense of self within relationships (Hobson, 1993; Stern, 1985). This work confirms the importance of the context of relationships to the development of self and identifies crucial aspects of personal relatedness that accompany it.

By including ideas about the social construction of gender with those of relationship, we can explore how these relationships and the emergence of selfhood are affected by beliefs about gender. Through scrutinizing theoretical writings and social arrangements in our society, feminists uncovered recurring patterns of gendered complementarity, with women and men placed differently and opposite each other in their experiences of selfhood. Everywhere—from childcare manuals to the psychoanalytic literature—mothers and women have been portrayed as people without desires or needs of their own, who were there to give recognition to others. Boys and men, on the other hand, were given a centrality of self and seen to have agency and desire (Benjamin, 1990). Recognizing that men and women had been described so differently in such writings means understanding that these writings not only reflect current ideas about selfhood but also influence them—i.e. "produce" experiences of selfhood.

An exploration of the connections between gender and subjectivity raises critical questions about essentialism and relativity. The idea that experiences of selfhood are "produced" challenges the notion that we each have a true essential self, the core of each of us. In the current climate of rapid social change, however, the wish to find and preserve the "authentic self" has become even more prevalent, as if it were a bulwark against overwhelming discontinuities; this discourse shapes and influences much popular psychology.

Our understanding that both gender and subjectivity are constructed leads us to another view—that our subjectivity is "dynamic and multiple, always positioned in relation to particular discourses and practices and produced by these" (Henriques, Hollway, Urwin, Venn, & Walkerdine, 1984, p. 3). (See Wetherell & White, 1992, for example, for an interesting discussion of four cultural narratives/discourses they identified, through which adolescent girls describe themselves when talking about eating and dieting.) In this view the "authentic self" is seen as itself "produced" rather than existing, waiting to be discovered. By exploring the ways in which traditional ideas of masculinity and feminity have supported stories of selfhood, we can identify the different implications of change for men and women. For men, this involves moving from a centrality of self to a more self-reflexive and multi-perspective position; for women, it means moving from a decentred position to one that includes more definition of self. Both of these moves open spaces for new experiences of self and relationship.

SELFHOOD AND MASCULINITY

One of the most common and therefore influential stories about selfhood in our Western culture has been that of the "unitary rational subject" (this is a term we first encountered in Henriques et al.'s work, 1984). This subject is a self with a coherent story who knows what he's about, what kind of person he is, how he got to where he is, and even where he might be going. And he definitely is a he, for men are assumed to be the unitary rational subject personified. To construct and maintain this sense of self, contradictory experiences, feelings, or ways of seeing things have to be dismissed or discounted and one main story of self becomes dominant, obscuring the process of its own construction. This account implicitly drew on the concept of the true essential self, which can be discovered independently of context or relationship.

For men, a sense of subjectivity has been centrally connected to a sense of masculinity. For boys, developing a strong sense of self, separate from their relationship with their mothers, has been viewed as crucial to their development and to their masculinity. Indeed, the descriptions of the construction of masculinity and the construction of the unitary rational subject involve similar processes. As we discussed in Chapter 1, masculinity is thought to be forged and constituted over and over again through its relationship with femininity. It continually needs to be reaffirmed and demonstrated through the maintainance of sexual polarities (Segal, 1990). It is this drive to assert a sense of masculinity that we think sharpens a sense of subjectivity.

However, this continual attempt to keep a centred subjectivity contains within it many dilemmas and hazards in managing selfhood and relationships, particularly in these times of rapid social change. Giddens (1992) sees men as having a much greater difficulty in reflecting on their selfhood, because their definition of self has been so bound up with issues of control and action. This is particularly complicated because it has involved being in control of women to whom they have given the power to define their sense of masculinity. As women reject that control, men face a crisis of selfhood. What Giddens goes on to argue is that men need to develop "communicative competence", with which to take into account and describe many of the experiences previously left out by them or dealt with by women. Being able to develop an observer position on themselves is a crucial aspect of this project which can helpfully be addressed in therapy.

SUBJECTIVITY AND FEMININITY

Women and selfhood have been described in rather different ways. Although femininity is defined as opposite to masculinity, it has sometimes been construed only as lack or gap and sometimes through its connection to nature. In any case, the onus has traditionally been more on men to prove their difference/their masculinity, rather than women their femininity. This is not to say that women do not worry about their femininity; indeed, traditionally they were expected to display femininity to procure and maintain a relationship with a male partner. But they have not needed to prove it in quite the same way. Traditionally, descriptions of gender have positioned women as object to men's subject. One struggle then has been how to own selfhood with agency, how to move from this decentred position.

With our current gendered arrangements, girls have not had to define their gendered selves in opposition to their mothers', and have lived lives where relationship and selfhood have not required differentiation in the way they have for males. The constraints and hazards of this kind of "production" of self came from the societal valuing of the unitary rational subject and the importance in certain contexts of the privileging of self over relationship. So, for example, in most work settings, clarity and purpose of self have been seen as more valuable than attention to relationships.

For many women who will have paid as much attention to their relationships as to themselves, their stories of self will have been produced through definitions offered by others, or through the giving of recognition to others. Some women will have experienced such extremes of objectification that only tenuous fragments of different experience survived, if at all (see Belenky, Clinchy, Goldberger, & Tarule, 1986, for research of a group of such women). Our argument here is that many women continually experience multiple realities and multiple subjectivities, but that there has not been a taboo against these, linked to gender identity, in the way there has for men. Thus, there has both been less "urgency", but also ultimately more difficulty in defining selfhood when certain contexts, such as a competitive organization, demand it.

MARGINALITY AND MULTIPLE SUBJECTIVITIES

Experiences of selfhood are also affected profoundly by race, class, and culture. Our view is that anyone defined by the dominant culture as "other" has faced similar contradictions of experiences to those we have described for women. This becomes even more complex when we consider different gendered experiences within any minority grouping. Experiences of self would then be produced in relation to different but overlapping contexts in which one found oneself—facing contradictions between one's own sense of oneself, how one is defined by others, and one's sensitivity to others (see bell hooks, 1991, and Lynne Segal, 1990, for interesting discussions of some of the contradictions faced by black men and women in Britain and the United States, and the challenges these make to concepts of selfhood and gender in our society generally.)

For women and people who, marginalized in Western societies, live lives of multiple realities at a number of different levels, finding a context in which these contradictory and often paradoxical experiences can be validated may be crucial. While the story of the unitary rational subject would not enable this, current ideas about the production of selves within relationships and within discourse can affirm multiple and contradictory realities.

Theoretical developments emerging from the study of women's experiences have been helpful in further challenging the traditional dichotomy between self and relationship. The Stone Centre authors (Jordan, Kaplan, Miller, Stiver, & Surrey, 1991), for example, turned on its head the traditional view that human growth of "the self" requires separation from others, to argue that what is required is the development of "a more complex sense of self within more complex relationships with other selves". The weakness of these writings lies in the way they describe "women's experiences" as primary, untouched by thought or values, as "essentialist". Thus instead of challenging gender difference, they contribute to its reinforcement. However, their work does open up different ways to think about both men and women's subjectivity and their relationships. Their re-thinking of the notion of empathy to include both thinking and feeling processes (Jordan et al., 1991) also helps dissolve unhelpful dichotomies between intuition and rationality.

CLINICAL APPLICATIONS

When we have included ideas about gendered self in our therapy, new thoughts have been generated. How does the woman see herself? Is she dominated by the sense others have of her? How does she manage contradictions between others' definitions of her and her own view, or indeed contradictions within her own experiences? How does the man see himself? Can he accept others' realities and views as valid and different from his own? How does he deal with ambiguities and contradictions within his own experiences and premises? How do these experiences affect and construct relationships? How do relationships ossify rigid gender patterns or allow for a creative exploration of difference? In what ways has feedback been different for males and females concerning their selfhood, and in which situations? Which aspects of self have been affirmed and developed, and which limited and constrained? In what ways can constraining contexts be changed to liberating ones? These questions address connections between individuals, their ideas about themselves, and their relationships.

Case example
"The tyranny of a belief in one truth"

In this case example, it was helpful to rethink a couple's dilemma in relation to the influence of the story of the unitary rational subject and the decentred woman.

A couple who had separated came to therapy about their daughter, who was chronically ill. They were worried that her distress about their relationship worsened her condition. Father had moved out to live with another woman, but there was still uncertainty about the future. Mother was very angry at being left, and Father felt very guilty about having left.

After a number of sessions, both parents decided it would be helpful to make a decision about their relationship for the sake of the children. Mother told Father that if he hadn't made a final decision by a certain date, she would take this to mean he would never return. Father became very distressed, saying he did not know what to do. At this point in the therapy, we decided to have a reflecting conversation (Andersen, 1987) about their dilemmas as we saw them. We thought Father believed that he needed to know the truth about why he had left home and what he *really* felt now, to be able to make a decision. As a result, he spent time reflecting carefully on his own thoughts and feelings, rather than those of others. However, the way he thought and felt about the situation kept changing, and there was a distinct possibility that there might be a number of different truths about the situation, rather than just the one. We saw mother meanwhile scanning the children and her husband rather than herself for an answer to the dilemma, and pushing for her husband to decide. We thought this might make it difficult for her to find out what would be right for her.

Addressing his belief in one truth faced this man with the challenge of a new notion of himself, but placed his dilemma in a different arena. The woman found the ideas about his preoccupation with self helpful and made the difficult move to finding out what she herself might need.

A rigidified gendered pattern of a man preoccupied with himself, and a woman offering recognition without asking for this in return, may be intensified if the man is struggling with a hazardous life event (see Chapter 7 for a more detailed case illustration of work with a couple in this situation). This can create extreme constraints for both individuals and their relationship.

The kinds of questions that invite people to think about their selves/themselves in a different way, what Tomm (1987) has called reflexive questions, can have a profound effect. For men, the task of becoming observers to themselves may be particularly difficult.

Mason (personal communication) will sometimes invite men to review the videotape of a session at home, in order to facilitate a more self-reflexive position. For some women in particular, who may always have been more aware of others and of relationships, questions that invite them to take themselves seriously, sometimes for the first time, may be crucial.

Case example
"The woman with panic attacks"

A woman asked for help regarding her severe panic attacks for which she had been hospitalized. She came to the first session saying she was terrified about being out of control. It emerged that she had left her violent husband a few years previously with her four children to live in a women's refuge. They had been rehoused, and she had managed to establish a new home with her children. With this information, it became possible to view her panic attacks as her ability to react and feel things about her separation, now that she was settled and strong enough. This new way to think about her panic attacks placed her in a different relationship to them. Instead of the attacks controlling her, she could see her feelings as legitimate. She was able to move from experiencing herself as an object to being a subject. Later in the interview, when the therapist asked her what she might want to do for herself in the future, there was a short pause—after which she said in a rather surprised way: "Do you know, I have never thought about myself."

This woman went on to take adult literacy classes and challenged ideas about herself held by her family and at school that she was someone who was unable to learn.

Women who have been in violent or abusive relationships may have particular difficulties in developing a sense of self at all, as they have experienced extreme conditions of being objectified. Perhaps what is most striking about these experiences and their effects is that they do not seem to challenge their own or others' views of their femininity. Indeed, such experiences seem, dangerously, to fit with traditional views of femininity, if at the extreme end of the continuum. The struggle towards developing a different story of self may therefore have to include challenging gender stereotypes, often held in implicit ways. This is particularly poignant when stereotypes are used "against" women by professionals. "You stay with him because you are masochistic." "You can't leave him because of your low self-esteem." We think this is very different to men's experiences of objectification.

MEN MANAGING POWERLESSNESS

For men, there seem to be particular challenges in managing ambiguity and facing contradictions. We believe this is particularly so in situations where men experience themselves as powerless and objectified. We suggest that these kinds of experiences pose contradictions for men at several different levels simultaneously, the most profound of which is at the level of beliefs about their selfhood and their masculinity.

Brian Keenan, writing about his experiences as a hostage in Lebanon, gives a vivid description of this process, within a context of extreme objectification by his captors. "During my captivity I, like my fellow hostages, was forced to confront the man I thought I was and to discover that I was many people. I had to befriend these many people, discover their origins, introduce them to each other and find a communality between themselves and myself" (Keenan, 1992, p. xv). He describes his supreme efforts to keep control of himself and his experiences and, then, the moment of giving up this fight for control and deciding to become his own self-observer, "allowing myself to do and be and say and think and feel all the things that were in me" (p. 78). Later, these experiences would be validated in his relationship with John McCarthy, who joined him in his cell.

In this situation, paradoxically as Keenan himself comments, finding "ourselves physically chained together we both realized an extraordinary capacity to unchain ourselves from what we had known and been—to set free those trapped people and parts of ourselves" (p. xvi). The fact that Keenan exposed his experiences to another man seen as his equal challenged traditional ideas about the intimacy allowed between men. This is a different experience from some men who expose their vulnerability to women and then feel they need to control them, in order to maintain a sense of their masculine invulnerability (see Chapters 5 and 6).

GENDERED IDENTITIES AS CONSTRAINTS

Our societal constructions of masculinity and feminity have proved problematic for both women's and men's sense of self. Becoming irreverent towards these constructions can be creative territory for couple and family therapy.

The connections between centrality of self and masculinity are worth exploring further. In our therapeutic work in the past, we often asked questions to elicit and highlight contradictions in family members' beliefs and between their beliefs and their behaviour, in order to present these as dilemmas. Now we are more aware of the effect this may have on some men in particular. To be asked to consider contradictions, when one has spent one's life attempting to banish these in constructing one's story, may prove too much of a contradiction!

Case example
"The man who hated being confused"

A separated couple came for therapy to decide whether they could get back together again. The husband presented a very fixed and stereotypic view of himself and his wife, saying, "I am all reason and she is all emotion." He wanted the therapist to interview each of them separately and to provide an objective assessment of their chances of reuniting. The wife complained that this was typical of his overbearing and controlling personality and the reason why she had wanted to leave him in the first place!

Our response to a request like this, which could put us in a bind as therapists, is sometimes to go ahead with separate interviews and then to have a reflecting conversation (Andersen, 1987) in front of the couple in which we present a number of different ideas and reflect on dilemmas. After some separate and conjoint sessions, the couple decided to get back together. Following this, the husband, in an individual session, talked about how confused he felt now his wife was back, because she was being so domineering and critical of him. He said, "I know I used to be a tyrant, but now she is just as bad."

When the therapist asked what was the worst thing about this experience for him, he said it was his sense of confusion; now the old certainties of the relationship were gone, he felt completely adrift. After discussing how unbearable he found this, the therapist raised the question of whether he could use the scientific side of him that he valued so much to think about the new situation. He did not think he could. The therapist suggested he thought of himself as like Albert Einstein, who went through a period of great confusion and uncertainty when nothing made sense, just before he developed his theory of relativity. Perhaps he could think of this as a similarly necessary prelude to a major creative breakthrough. Following this session and in subsequent joint sessions, the couple developed their relationship in a much less constrained way.

For women in relationships, the dilemma is often the reverse. When they have defined themselves through others, the process of paying attention to feedback from themselves in different contexts, particularly if this flies in the face of others' ideas, can be very difficult. Sometimes this only happens after a relationship has broken down, and women need to manage themselves and their children in a different way and discover different versions of self (see Burck & Daniel, 1994).

The gender of the therapist is an important element in these discussions. If a man is invited to consider contradictions in his premises by a male therapist who can position himself more personally in relation to discourses about masculinity, this may have considerable impact. If a female therapist invites a man to do the same, can she avoid being seen as yet another woman who is inviting him to become more like her. If a male therapist invites a woman to become irreverent about femininity, will she take this as yet another way in which she is being defined by a male?

DEVELOPING INTER-SUBJECTIVE RELATIONSHIPS

A relationship between two people involves balancing the tension between recognizing the other's experiences and views and asserting one's own. When can conflicting interests be reframed to become collaborative ones without being a cover-up? This requires a shift in paradigm from the dominator model (Eisler, 1987) in which relationships and differences of gender, race, and class are constructed in terms of inequality. Although we almost agree with Benjamin (1990), who says that none of us really knows what equal relationships would look like, we believe there are many relationships in our society, not currently valued, that offer variations and possibilities. Friendships, we have argued elsewhere (Burck, Daniel, Kearney, & Mason 1992), although open to the possibilities of replicating dominator patterns, are one such context; gay and lesbian relationships where gender difference does not structure relationships may be another (Giddens, 1992; Salt, Bor, & Palmer, 1994; Segal, 1990).

COHERENCE AND CONTRADICTIONS

At the present time in our culture and history, people are facing rapid and fundamental political and social changes, and need to manage a constant bombardment of pluralities of views. The tasks facing us are how to manage the contradictions and ambiguities of rapidly shifting contexts. We are curious about the connections between coherence and contradictions, and the tensions this may create for women and men. Antonovsky (1992) has suggested that at this time of rapid social change, we will rely more on coherences offered by the state, religion, economics, or a belief in "the family", which in turn shape our subjectivities. He warns of the dangers of giving up complexity and contradiction.

A sense of coherence is helpful in providing a framework for meaning-making and has been found to be connected to an ability to survive change and trauma. Recent research exploring parents' accounts of their own lives, for example, found that a sense of coherence, rather than the kinds of experiences, correlated with positive relationships with their firstborn (Steele et al., 1993)

These different views indicate to us that there are inherent tensions in maintaining coherence. Attempting to maintain coherence of patterns of belief and behaviour may involve denying many contradictions. On the other hand, coherence at the level of seeing patterns *in* contradictions may allow for the validation of ambiguity and fragmentation. Contradictions and coherence can connect to each other in a process over time: developing a coherence of self may enable the managing of many contradictions, and experiences of ambiguity and inconsistencies may lead to a different and multiple sense of self.

Some persons who experience irreconcilable contradictions have constructed their subjectivity as a number of different selves, as multiple personalities, so that each personality has a coherence. This process has mainly become defined as pathological by professionals and persons themselves.

Case example
"How can two be company?"
A woman who had suffered horrific sexual abuse from her father when she was a child came for therapy. She had tried many times to disclose, had run away from home, and finally had left to live virtually on the streets, turning to drugs and prostitution, without her family ever acknowledging that the abuse had occurred. She developed two different "selves", one of which was highly competent, articulate, and socially skilled, and another personality that derided everything she did in the world, censored her conversation in therapy, and urged her to commit self-harming acts. In therapy she and the therapist struggled with how to develop a relationship between these two selves. However, she was profoundly affected by the belief that, although developing another "separate" self was a logical response to her experience of violation, she ought, "as most people did", to have just one true self. She struggled hard to overcome her sense of being doubly condemned to be an outsider, firstly by the abuse, and secondly by the psychological means she had used to survive.

The certainties of self, traditionally derived from family ties and stable work environments, are no longer secure. This can lead to a "more-of-the-same" response to experiences of incoherence, by attempts to find and maintain the "real me" (Gergen, 1991). What may be more useful would be the development of coherent-enough narratives of self negotiated over and over again in the context of different relationships and discourses. With our current gendered arrangements, girls brought up as experts on relationships may be better equipped to do this than boys, who have been more preoccupied with issues of control over relationships than with learning about them. Women may then find themselves holding contradictory expectations: on the one hand, communities see them as providers of stability in these times of trauma and rapid change; on the other, they frequently carry the potential and push for change.

CHAPTER 4

Gender, power, and systemic thinking

> "All power is unstable.... There is never power, but only a race for power. Power is, by definition, only a means... but power-seeking, owing to its essential incapacity to seize hold of its object, rules out all consideration of an end, and finally comes... to take the place of all ends."
>
> Simone Weil (1934)

Finding ways to conceptualize power in systemic therapy has been one of the most challenging issues in the last ten years and it has given rise to some moving and liberating therapy as well as some spectacular evasions. We find it ironic that the debate about power is often still referred to as the "Bateson/Haley debate", although the two men exchanged no more than a couple of sentences on the subject in 1976, and the terms of their difference were limited to the sterile question of whether power does or does not exist. Evidence from feminist therapists that it does indeed exist and has to be thought about is met by accusations of lineal thinking, and neat (and equally lineal) catch-phrases have sprung from constructivist lips such as "Power is created by submission" (Maturana, quoted in Mackinnon & Miller, 1987). Posing the question in this way, it seems to us, limits the possibilities for thinking systemically about the experience of domination and oppression. We believe that feminist thinking offers as many challenges to a lineal view of power as does cybernetics.

We need to distinguish the question "Does power exist?" (to which we could only answer a resounding Yes!) from the questions "Do we therefore have to be organized into believing that relationships based on power and domination are inevitable?" and "What are the contexts that sustain this belief and how does it affect our thinking and practice?"

We consider that it is important to think about power at different, mutually interacting levels and to consider the further question: "How can systemic thinking help us address the paradoxes of power in society and in intimate relationships?" We think that, at both these levels, the use or abuse of power and the belief in power and control are inextricably linked and that beliefs about power are invariably gendered.

Therefore, to stay with the question of whether power exists is to reduce power to an objective "thing" rather than a social construction and an interactive process. We also think that ideas about power that equate it only with a repressive force, or conceive of it in terms of the material world, are very constraining on therapists and are more likely to lead to denial of power and thus a potential abuse of therapy.

While radical constructivist positions on power can lead to a denial of the inequality and oppression many people experience in their daily lives, we think that the position on power taken by Bateson (1972), when he linked belief in power to the attempt to exert unilateral control, is in some respects close to the thinking of many feminists. Bateson's position is very interesting and has to some extent been misrepresented as well as limited by his failure to place his argument in any kind of socio-political context.

Paul Dell (1989) drew attention to two main issues in Bateson's position on power. The first is the idea, which Bateson propounded forcefully and passionately, that belief in power is an epistemological error, because it is a concept derived from the material world which has no part in human relationships. He proposed that a belief in power leads inevitably to disaster both in intimate relationships and for our planet. This belief he described as "epistemological lunacy". Many feminists writers have reached, by rather different routes, similar conclusions to Bateson's view that belief in power is an epistemological error (Benjamin, 1990; Eisler, 1987; French, 1986).

The second issue is Bateson's suggestion that, because no part of an interactive system can have unilateral control over any other, power therefore cannot exist in the real world. The latter assertion is the one that some systems writers have taken up most enthusiastically when they contend that, given a circular epistemology, the metaphor of power is an irrelevance and constrains our thinking (Keeney, 1983). Dell (1989) points out that Bateson's views about the pathogenicity of power have been overshadowed by his other claim: that because the concept of power involves a false and lineal epistemology, it is therefore impossible and cannot exist. In viewing power as pathogenic, Bateson is taking a moral as much as a scientific position, as he passionately believed that using the metaphor of power was anti-ecological, "productive of ugliness and destruction".

If we return to the second half of Bateson's argument—that because the concept of power involves a false and lineal epistemology, it is therefore impossible and cannot exist—we can see how his argument is limited by its acontextual nature. This has given rise to most criticism by feminists because of his apparent denial that there are victims of the abuse of power and his implication that we cannot, within a systemic epistemology, find an intellectually respectable way of describing structures of inequality and oppression that put some people in stronger and weaker positions of power. We do not believe that Bateson's step—i.e. from belief in power as a false epistemology to a dismissal of the experience of power in the real world—is an inevitable or even a logical one. The problem is how to describe power structures, coercive relationships, or experiences of oppression without becoming so organized by these discourses that we talk about them as if they were structural "givens".

To manage this we have to make a distinction of levels: that which we analyse—i.e. power structures, oppressive processes— and that of our critical stance on the discourses within which these processes are embedded. In our discussion of this topic, we take a position that moves between these two levels. We believe that systemic thinking, far from making it "impossible to pose . . . questions about the nature of a system itself" (James & McIntyre, 1983), provides us with extremely useful tools with which to manage this complex task.

In doing this we are making a different distinction to the one Dell (1989) makes when he attempts to deal with Bateson's dismissal of the the existence of power. Dell puts forward the idea that there is a difference between the realm of scientific explanation, the context in which Bateson is operating, and the realm of description, which deals with that which is experienced. Dell argues that to describe an act of violence or abuse as one person exercising power over another is a correct, indeed an essential punctuation of human experience, but a scientific explanation, to be adequate, would need to take into account all the contextual variables, and thus provide a more recursive explanation of the action. However, this proposition of Dell's does not seem to be adequate or satisfactory. Firstly, it does not address the recursive relationship between belief in power and control and violent or coercive behaviour. Secondly, it does not specify where this realm of scientific explanation is located; the implication is that it occupies some kind of neutral zone, independent of the observer, where all forms of power are equal and such moral dilemmas do not exist.

Here it is important to remind ourselves of the context for the observer/writer. For Bateson and his followers—mainly white, male, and privileged—inequalities of power, status, and resources were not burning issues that were experienced at a personal level. Furthermore, we would argue that Bateson did in fact ascribe enormous power to women when he described the "double-binding" behaviour of mothers of schizophrenics, which he considered led to the young person being driven into psychotic behaviour. This, as Luepnitz (1988) has speculated, may well relate to Bateson's fear and resentment of his own mother. Perhaps Bateson's own source of power came to be his power of mind and ideas, to the extent that he could blithely make the move from finding an idea (of power) morally repugnant to believing that it therefore does not exist!

What Bateson failed to see, probably because he was not challenged to take a critical stance on his gendered experience, was the extent to which belief in power stems from such experience. Feminist writers, on the other hand, have deconstructed concepts such as power by placing them in the context of history, developmental psychology, and gendered experience. Bateson has been criticized for neglecting a historical perspective in his work (Luepnitz, 1988), which is an interesting omission given that he believed in the social and contextual nature of ideas.

Two feminist writers have been particularly illuminating in providing a historical analysis of power and in placing gender at the centre of that analysis. Marilyn French (1985) and Riane Eisler (1987) have each critiqued power as a construct of patriarchy.

French argues that, historically, a belief in power has been as enslaving of men as it has of women. She traces chronologically the ways men have exerted power over women in all spheres of life, and the way belief in power and control was one of the factors that maintained this state of affairs. Belief in absolute power, and the anxiety experienced when this power is felt to be slipping away, is often what leads tyrants, whether domestic or national, to excesses of domination. The quest for power is also "the drive . . . to transcendence: the accomplishment by humans of a God-like invulnerability . . . the ability to affect others without being affected ourselves". French argues that is false to talk about "having power" because it is inevitably an interactive process, not a "thing" that can be possessed. "It is always true that those whom we control, or seek to control, also control us." French's argument that the attainment of absolute power is thus an impossibility and that the quest for power is a corrupting and self-reinforcing process echoes both our clinical experience and our experience as citizens.

Riane Eisler, in her book *The Chalice and the Blade* (1987), also explores the history of human society and the ways in which "dominator" cultures (those based on autocracy and conflict) have superseded "partnership" cultures (those based on peaceful cooperation). This has happened to such an extent that we now believe that dominator cultures are the only ones that can exist. She equates the two types of culture with societies based on male domination and societies based on equality between the sexes. She calls the first "andocracy" (rule by men) and uses the word "gylany", a word that has elements of male and female in it, to describe the second. She deliberately does not use the word patriarchy, because it implies an opposite—matriarchy. Because we have become so accustomed to dominator models, we assume that societies that were not ruled by men must have been ruled by women. Thus, when evidence of non-patriarchal societies began to emerge in the nineteenth century, they were assumed to be matriarchies; when evidence of matriarchy was not forthcoming, this was seen as proof that human society was, and always would be, ruled by men.

Eisler argues that authoritarian and repressive societies throughout the world have always been those which are rigidly male-dominated (andocratic). When gylanic (i.e. more cooperative, peaceful) societies have emerged, they have always been characterized by better treatment of women and an espousal of "feminine" values. She argues that our present time is one where there is the potential for a major "gylanic thrust" because of increasing awareness of the threat to the global ecology, and she cites the increasing public face of women, the number of agencies devoted to international cooperation, and the thinking associated with cybernetics and the new physics. However, she also argues that, whenever female voices and feminine values have been in the ascendance, this is responded to by an upsurge of male violence towards women and an increase in repression.

There are many indications of this, from the growth of fundamentalist religious movements, most of which are highly restrictive of women, to the punitive policies in this country towards single mothers. Susan Faludi, in her book *Backlash* (1991), has written about the negative reaction to feminism among the new right in the United States under the guise of promoting "family values". Given that increasing numbers of women are occupying positions of power in Western society and are thus less likely to be attacked directly, this "backlash" may take place at different levels of the system. For example, the media give coverage to murders of women far more often than murders of men, which are in fact more numerous, and this leads to exhortations to women to keep off the streets at night "for their own safety". Judith Walkowitz (1984) argues that the way that Peter Sutcliffe, the "Yorkshire Ripper", was portrayed by the press amplified the threat of male violence towards women, presented the cities as dangerous places for women, and indirectly buttressed male authority over women.

We can also see this process in couple relationships with large increases in the incidence of domestic violence, often sparked off by pathological jealousy, one reason for which being men's jealousy of relationships their wives might be having when they were at work. "The sexual control of women by men", argues Anthony Giddens (1992), "is more than an incidental feature of modern social life. As that control starts to break down, we see the compulsive character of male sexuality more plainly revealed—and this declining control also generates a rising tide of male violence towards women." If women's empowerment is viewed within this paradigm of dominator/dominated, then it is clearly more threatening than if it were viewed as a development that could benefit men and society generally.

If we are to understand how beliefs about power at the societal level are reflected at the personal and interactional level, then we need to think of power not only as a repressive force, but also as constitutive—i.e. to understand how we come to participate in maintaining these power structures. Michel Foucault (1980) writes that, whereas our conception of power is usually that of a negative or oppressive force, contributing to repression, it can be seen to have a positive effect. By positive he does not mean beneficial, but in the creation of a narrative through which people construct their lives. In this way, power and knowledge become inseparably linked, as the ascendancy and acceptance of certain knowledges leads to the silencing and disqualification of others.

Feminists have highlighted the ascendancy of a "male" ideology with its emphasis on hierarchy, competitiveness, abstract rules, and loyalty to institutions over intimate personal relationships. Foucault's argument for the need to challenge the enslaving idea of a unitary truth, recover subjugated knowledges, and develop a multiplicity of views is closely connected to his belief that such unitary truths serve as vehicles of power. Feminist analyses of the gender base of power include the constitutive as well as the repressive aspects of power. Part of the dominant ideology that feminists critique is precisely the belief in repressive power and its inevitability.

Viewing power in this way avoids the need to make the kind of artificial distinction between the realms of description and scientific explanation that Dell uses. Both can be seen as part of a recursive pattern where the behaviour of the oppressor and of the oppressed is shaped by dominant narratives about power.

Our understanding of the process whereby men and women constrain themselves by explicitly or implicitly accepting received ideas about "gender-acceptable" behaviour is facilitated by Foucault's notion concerning "power through truth". This leads to a specification of a form of individuality which itself becomes a vehicle of power. Foucault argues that individuals are controlled through being categorized and documented in relation to specific norms. Individuals participate in their own subjugation by also defining and categorizing themselves in relation to these norms (e.g. by accepting the label "depressive"). Our lives are "captured and fixed in writing" as a form of social control in which we are evaluated in relation to social norms or levels of performance.

The recursive nature of this process thus lies in the way people become involved in the policing of their own behaviour. "He [sic] who is subjected to a field of visibility, and who knows it, assumes responsibility for the constraints of power; he makes them play spontaneously upon himself; he inscribes himself in the power relation in which he simultaneously plays both roles; he becomes the principle of his own subjugation" (quoted in White, 1989). This is particularly relevant to understanding the way sex roles confine both women and men in monitoring their own behaviour, which then perpetuates sex-role socialization as a vehicle of domination.

A way of understanding power and domination as a recursive process can thus lie in identifying those beliefs about power which serve to organize the behaviour of oppressor and oppressed and which can go some way towards understanding women's "participation" in their oppression. We have identified three major beliefs about power that can be seen, in Foucault's sense, to be constitutive of a narrative about power. In order to understand how these narratives are constructed at the personal level, it is useful to review the contributions that feminist pychologists have made to our understanding of the development of a gender identity.

Women's power and the power of nature

Time and again in literature and mythology, we encounter a belief in the "fundamental nature" of women's power and its equation with the power of the natural world, a power that then needs to be subject to control and domination. Alongside this belief is the paradox that, however terrible are the repressive systems that might be set up to control and dominate woman/nature, they are bound to be ephemeral and are therefore permanently vulnerable.

Dorothy Dinnerstein (1976) sees the origin of men's desire to dominate women in the infantile experience of being given birth to and brought up by a woman and thus experiencing women as having the power over life and death. Because men cannot identify with this powerful person on whom they are at the same time so helplessly dependent, this creates a fear of women's power which is dealt with by attempts to dominate and control women. Dinnerstein argues that the fear of women generalizes to all that is instinctual and is a psychological explanation for men's wish to control and exploit the natural world.

Camille Paglia makes a similar point to Dinnerstein when she says in typically graphic fashion that:

> Male bonding and patriarchy were the recourse to which man was forced by his terrible sense of women's power, her imperviousness, her archetypal confederacy with chthonic nature. . . . Woman is the primeval fabricator, the first real mover. She turns a gob of refuse into a spreading web of sentient being, floating on the snaky umbilical by which she leashes every man. [Paglia, 1991, p. 12]

Although this passage is quoted by Cecchin et al. (1992) in order to challenge the "radical feminist notion that women are the victims of men", what Paglia's passage makes explicit is the association of woman with nature. This portrayal of women's power connects the idea of society as a defence against nature with that of patriarchy as a way of suppressing women's power.

A notorious example of the way myths about women's power can be used as a means of social control is from the Moynihan report on the "Black Family" in America, when, rather than looking at the effect of racism and poverty, the problem he highlights is the "abnormal" black family structure in which women are too powerful and "impose a crushing burden on the Negro male". Wallace (1987) argued that this belief that black women are castrating and domineering led men to an assertion of "black macho", which further dissipated the possibility of challenging the white establishment. Bryan, Dadzie, and Scafe (1985) wrote about black men's violence towards women in Britain: "Black men's oppression of us is merely a façade of power... the domestic arena has become the only area in which men are able to conform to the dominant male role."

It is important to point out that, when we talk about the "myth" of women's power, we are not denying that women can and do wield power. To claim that women are powerless would be to fall into the same reductionist trap as to believe in absolute power. Societies where women are most excluded from positions of power or status in public life are often ones where they are seen as wielding enormous power in the domestic arena. They may thus be experienced as domineering by their children, as jokes about "Jewish mothers" reveal. There seems to be an interesting relationship between feelings of powerlessness and attempts to dominate in other contexts. This relationship is frequently observed in couples' interactions around violence (see Chapter 6).

One dilemma that faces therapists is that when women's power is seen as potentially overwhelming and toxic, women may feel much safer in taking a view of themselves as powerless and will thus be less likely to own their power. This fear of women's power provides a good "fit" with another belief: that men are basically rather fragile and need to be protected. This may be a particular issue in societies where men are more in contact with, and therefore more vulnerable to, the wider socio-economic context and its vagaries than women and have a sense of self that is much more bound up with status in that world.

Women's self-image may be less threatened by oppression in the wider society because their self-image has not been tied to external power and status in the way that men's have. Women who attack and belittle men when they are failing to "make it" in the outside world as providers for their family may be acting upon very rigid gendered beliefs that lead them to be ambivalent about their own power and, paradoxically, to attempt to recreate men's power. We are also interested in how women experience their power in familial and social contexts where there are few close and dependable male role models available. (See the first case study in Chapter 7 for a further elaboration of this theme.)

Power as a "finite thing"

The belief that if one person "has" power, another does not, means that the empowerment of those in subordinate positions poses a threat that may be counteracted by further use of power. Just as Eisler (1987) noted that the only alternative form of society to patriarchy is usually assumed to be matriarchy, so a pervasive belief is that if women have more power, men will have less. This links with the issue of women denying their power or keeping it secret because they, too, may be organized by this belief. Jean Baker Miller (1976), in her analysis of how dominant/subordinate positions affect men's and women's intimate relationships, describes how men often respond to women's attempts to gain more power by acting as if this was an attempt to steal something from them and as if they would inevitably be losers. We can see this process in contexts where comments about women "wearing the trousers" are used about women asserting themselves over very minor issues. We often hear how men are "emasculated" by feminism. Power and powerlessness are thus construed as polarized opposites, and the prevailing paradigm about power is unchallenged.

Even in contexts where women are seen as powerful, we still see constraints operating for women if they fear that, by pushing too hard for their own self-advancement, they will somehow be depriving men of a diminishing resource. This belief, as Jean Baker Miller (1976) points out, may have the effect of leading women to develop more indirect ways of seeking power (e.g. behaviour that she describes as "psychological sabotage of the male"). This, in turn, may lead to women's power being more feared because it is "underhand" and secret or because it is expressed in the form of personal attacks.

Power means autonomy

The third belief is the relationship between power and autonomy and the desire on the part of those with power to deny their own weakness and vulnerability, which becomes vested in the subordinate who must therefore be subject to control. Jessica Benjamin, in *The Bonds of Love* (1990), describes domination in relation to the denial of dependent, vulnerable aspects of self which men cannot own because they are associated with womanhood and because they would challenge a male myth about autonomy. These qualities then become invested in women, but, because they can neither be owned nor disregarded, they have to be subject to control, which means the control of women. Benjamin draws a parallel with the fact that in most Western capitalist societies the "feminine" qualities of caring and nurturance, at once despised and necessary, are devalued and kept primarily in the private domain. Eisler (1987) describes these as "the co-operative activities that permit the now over-rewarded competitive activities to appear successful".

In their work with violent couples, Goldner et al. (1990) describe the way in which the team "deconstructs" the violent moment for the man and the woman. What emerges from the men is generally an account of the violence occurring at the moment when they are most overwhelmed by feelings of vulnerability and dependence on the woman. These feelings are often triggered by a fear of loss, either when the woman expresses an independent view or when she threatens to leave. The paradox in this process is that men may want to control women in order that women will affirm them in their sense of masculinity, but, if women do this, it only increases men's sense of women's power. As discussed earlier, masculinity cannot be taken for granted, because it is based on disidentification with the caretaking parent and therefore has to be reinvented every day. Men have to be exhorted to "Be men", women only to "Be grown up". Reinventing masculinity daily could be a wearisome project that keeps women irritably accomodating to the men in their lives and denying their own subjectivity rather than face the possibility of degendering half the population of the world. Perhaps that is the "terrible secret" of women's power described by Camille Paglia?

Colleagues from Eastern Europe and the former Soviet Union (Gjuricova and Purvaneckiene, personal communication 1992) have commented on a resurgence of patriarchy in the wake of the collapse of Communism, with both men and women expressing a preference for traditional family forms and dismissing feminist thinking. Although the reasons for this are complex and multifacetted, including the mistrust of any "ideology", one explanation is that heading the traditional family provides a context for men to experience some sense of a masculinity eroded by the Communist state and subsequently by economic disruption and mass unemployment and that women work hard to maintain them in this position.

Thus, our understanding of the relationship between power and gender has to do justice to complexity, to the different levels in which power is embedded, and to the recursive processes through which beliefs about power and the exercise of power interact. This also enables us to understand the processes of empowerment and change in more complex ways. Foucault and therapists who have been particularly influenced by his thinking (White & Epston, 1990) describe empowerment in terms of the recovery of subjugated knowledges.

We can see that a process of this kind took place in the consciousness-raising groups, which were a prime feature of the women's movement; they provided a context from which to evaluate critically the dominant narrative, to challenge belief systems that held women as participants in their own oppression, and to create alternative stories.

In the political sphere, an example of how a change in the belief about power affects the nature of that power, despite the "objective" reality of power imbalances, can be seen in the collapse of Communism in Eastern Europe and the former Soviet Union. The speed with which previously all-powerful leaders and party machines were challenged and then toppled can be seen both as a reflection of the way the people came to view their own power differently in relation to their leaders, and the way the leaders themselves came to view the people's ability to demand and insist on change, and thus they abdicated their positions in a hitherto unimaginable fashion.

Any analysis of power that does not take into account how change can take place in unpredictable ways, when new attitudes and beliefs are shaped by new experiences of empowerment and in turn create completely new recursive patterns around power, is in our view inadequate. An analysis of power only as a "structural given" can be a restricting way of thinking for feminists, because it does not allow for the possibility of change. This is not to deny the historical realities of women's oppression, nor to believe in a feminist utopia where women's values predominate and men give up their dominating competitive ways, and power is no longer an issue.

Rather, it is that when we maintain a critical edge on beliefs about power and understand the constraints on our thinking and actions that stem from our relationship to the dominant culture, then we can position ourselves to think about what is missing, pose the outrageous question, and believe in the possibility of empowerment.

The illusory nature of power and the dangers inherent in beliefs about unilateral power are as much challenged by feminist as by systemic perspectives. One of the most important contributions feminist scholars have made is that they have elevated the argument beyond a debate about whether or not relationships are inevitably based on power, to the level of observing the ways in which our thinking about power has been shaped and constrained by the particular context (i.e. patriarchy) that we inhabit. This above all enhances rather than detracts from a systemic view of the world. In Chapter 5, we describe how we apply some of these ideas clinically when we work with abuses of power in families.

CHAPTER 5

Abuses of power: working with physical and sexual violence

While power is an ever-present dimension of gender relations, it is when we face issues of physical and sexual abuse that we confront power in its rawest form. Although this chapter is primarily about physical violence, we include some ideas about working with sexual abuse.

Until recently family therapists have mainly ignored violence; families tended not to volunteer the information and therapists tended not to persist in asking. Men were likely to deny either the occurrence or the seriousness of the violence; women feared retaliation outside the session or were inhibited by a sense of loyalty or shame. If violence has been a continuous feature of family life, a couple may not even have seen it as relevant to the problem for which they sought therapy. It is extremely difficult to remain neutral in the face of violence, and it is unethical to be neutral to the act itself. We agree with Wiesel who says: "neutrality helps the oppressor, never the victim" (quoted in Keeney & Bobele, 1989). We take a view that one aim of the work is always to stop the violence. However, the other issue is how therapists can hear different subjective accounts of the violence.

In our work we try to hold a position that allows us to take sides against violence but, at the same time, uses an understanding of the constraining and brutalizing nature of a violent interaction to help address what participating in it does to both abuser and abused. In this way we hope to help men own responsibility for their use of violence and to expect them to stop it. We aim to help women to identify the circumstances that contributed to their involvement with men who were violent to them. For both men and women, exploring beliefs about power and control is an important part of this process.

VIOLENCE AND SOCIETY

We think it important to define what we mean by violence—the use of physical force with intent to threaten or physically hurt someone else. In our culture, physical violence is often equated with other types of abuse, but we have found it helpful to consider physical violence as a category on its own. There have always been questions about what constitutes violence and in what context. Although slapping a child—at least if you don't leave a bruise—is often not seen as abuse or violence in Britain and the United States, doing so to an adult is (Gelles, 1985). Some actions permitted inside the family would not be tolerated in any other context (Straus & Gelles, 1988). And violence is legitimated by the state in certain contexts, such for the army or the police. This again highlights the importance of beliefs and context on the definition, meanings, and interactions around violence.

A number of the premises on which our society is founded can be seen as instrumental in condoning violence in our culture. There is a common belief about the usefulness of pain. Violence towards children was seen as necessary and educative: "spare the rod and spoil the child". Although these beliefs have changed, we still live in a culture where violence is condoned for educational purposes. Society now steps in when parents bruise their children, but many parents still believe that slapping children is one of the only effective ways to control them, despite evidence to the contrary (Burgess & Youngblade, 1988). Parents often describe their children as attempting to show that physical punishment does not affect them in the least ("that didn't hurt"), which only further exasperates them as they still feel they do not have control. Many films and TV programmes reinforce the idea that one denies pain to get peer approval and to get back at others' attempts to control. These beliefs often reappear in couples relationships. Work with a woman who had recently left a violent relationship revealed that she felt that she should be "big enough to take this", just as she had when she was a child.

The idea that the woman is responsible for the man's violence towards her links to the belief that women deserve to be hit by men. Although most of us now strongly disagree with this, until the nineteenth century, in Western culture, men had a right, if not a duty, to punish their wives with physical force for not carrying out their marital responsibilities (Dobash & Dobash, 1979). This social construction has only recently been challenged through changes in the legal system, with rape in marriage now illegal. A survey of men in prison for violent and/or sexual attacks on women found that they overwhelmingly held the women responsible for what had happened (Ptacek, 1988). In our clinical work, we find that women, too, often believe this. Serra (1993) also describes how the way violence is constructed leaves women who have been beaten describing themselves as the accused who feel guilt-ridden.

The impression that it is women who feel they need to justify themselves may account for the long and excessively detailed narratives many women give of all the actions, however seemingly trivial, committed against them by their partners. It is as if they are on the defensive, having to justify their sense of violation.

VIOLENCE IN COUPLES RELATIONSHIPS

As we saw in the previous chapter, the beliefs in power and control in society can be replicated in intimate relationships. The more a man sees a need to be dominant as central to his self-esteem and identity, the more he may require confirmation for this belief in all his family interactions. If other ways to see himself as competent are reduced or he feels powerless in the outside world (e.g. through unemployment), any challenge, however minor, from another family member may be experienced as a deliberate attack on his self-image. This may lead to violence as an attempt to obtain or regain control (Ferraro, 1988).

Women are often influenced by the belief that they should be sensitive to their partner's needs and should be responsible for the emotional well-being of the family. They may then feel responsible if things go wrong, even if they do not know what will trigger the violence. There is a recursive pattern between beliefs and also one between experiences of power and powerlessness. We find it useful clinically to explore each partner's experience of power and powerlessness, because we realize that when a person feels most powerless in a transaction, that person may come across as most powerful. For example, a man whose partner is trying to remove herself from a situation that is escalating dangerously may feel totally powerless because he cannot keep her; his behaviour will, of course, come across to her as extremly powerful. If, on the other hand, he is trying to walk out, possibly to get himself under control, and she tries to stop him, she may be feeling powerless because she is failing to manage the relationship, but she will probably be experienced by him as extremely powerful.

There are often periods immediately after violence when the man engages the woman in a very different way; he is remorseful and promises to give up his violence. The couple may feel intensely and passionately close at this time (Goldner et al., 1990). This pattern often has the effect of keeping both the man and the woman involved with each other despite the violence. Goldner et al. have emphasized the importance of the positive bond between the man and the woman in keeping them together in the face of family and professional disapproval.

Physical abuse is often only one part of a pattern of threats, intimidation, coercion, and manipulation that the batterer employs to achieve dominance. Work with men on controlling their anger has been criticized because it may teach men how to control women in nonviolent ways, when the problem lies in their belief that it is possible and necessary to control others unilaterally.

MEN'S AND WOMEN'S VIOLENCE

Although, given its predominance, we are mainly addressing male violence, it is useful to look at differences between male and female batterers. Some women do hit their male partners (usually with considerably less damage) and women do physically abuse children. However, women have more to lose if they are violent to men. In general, they are weaker and could end up physically more hurt. The use of violence is also inconsistent with beliefs about femininity and maternity. Indeed, violent women get longer custodial sentences when violent to men than vice-versa.

Both men and women will be influenced by the factor of their relative strengths and size. These physical differences will interact with other factors like the sanctions against girls and women being physically aggressive and those that support and encourage these behaviours in boys and men. If the man is seen as stronger and able to cause physical damage, he is more likely to be given and to take power in this area. Often the threat of violence will be enough to influence the interactions between members in the family. Serra (1993) argues that male and female non-violence, too, has very different meanings: with males this is seen as a moral choice, with females, because it is taken as a sign of powerlessness, non-violence does not carry the same moral connotation.

THERAPEUTIC WORK WITH VIOLENCE AND ABUSE

We have worked with couples conjointly, as well as with women on their own, when there has been violence. Like other practitioners (Goldner et al., 1990), we think that conjoint work has its place in work with violence, although we always keep open the option to see either partner individually. We always try to address the societal beliefs and the context in which the abusive relationship is taking place. We do this by asking questions to highlight for ourselves the beliefs that may be influencing them.

There is evidence that abusive men are not motivated to seek treatment unless there are strong external pressures to do so. One of the most effective pressures may be the woman threatening to or actually leaving the relationship. This can also be one of the most dangerous for the woman, as evidenced by the need for women's refuges to keep addresses secret and the oft-used threat of murder if the woman actually tries to leave the field.

Some men face profound dilemmas over considering and giving validity to others' views and beliefs about the world. In taking on others' positions as valid and different from their own, men can no longer act as if their own views are paramount and all-encompassing. This shows up in its most extreme form in relationships where men abuse. It is often connected to a change in their status when their power or ability to block or misinterpret feedback has been challenged.

Case example
"What was the worst thing for your daughter?"

In work with the family of origin of an adult woman who had been sexually abused by her father, where she did not feel able to tell him about her experience of his abuse, we decided to ask her father a series of questions about his daughter's experiences of him at the time. Questions included what he thought she as a child would have hoped for from him; what he thought the worst thing was for her about the abuse; and how this might still be affecting how she related to him now. Although this man found it extremely difficult to answer these questions, when the therapist persisted in engaging with him about his daughter's experience, he was able to start to think about this as different from what he had wanted to imagine. His answers also allowed his daughter to begin to have her own experiences of the abuse validated without her having to challenge him directly.

This kind of questioning can challenge abusers to consider the experiences of those they abuse, to give subjectivity to those they have turned into objects, and can therefore contribute to lessening possibilities of further abusing. It also enables those who have been abused to reclaim their own experiences and selves, as the therapy allows those descriptions which the original abuse denied.

WORK WITH WOMEN ON THEIR OWN

Case example
"If the boot were on the other foot?"

In work with a woman with five children, who had a partner who came and went in the family, it took some time before she talked about his violence. The therapist used a question that shifted the context in an unexpected way for the client.

Shirley: ... and then Dan punched me.

Therapist: How do you explain why he did that?

Shirley: It was because of my jealousy ... er, I always ask him who he's been with.

Therapist: And why is it that he should choose to hit you?

(*Shirley then talked about believing that she deserved to be hit. Her mother had also been violently abused by her father over long periods of time while she had been growing up.*)

Therapist: What would Dan have to do which would make you feel that he deserved to be hit by you?

(*Shirley looked quite stunned, then laughed*).

Following this session, she, for the first time, called the police and had her partner evicted from the house when he became violent. Following a second instance when he started to threaten violence and she called the police, her partner stopped his abuse. Some couple work was then done.

Some women may find it very difficult to make changes in their relationship to violence because of powerful intergenerational patterns; therapy can be helpful in generating new perspectives on these (see also the first case study in Chapter 7).

Case example
"Do you deserve better?"
A woman, Ms Matthew, with a young child asked for help because, although she had tried to leave a very violent relationship, she found herself returning. The dilemmas for her had become even more acute since the involvement of social services, who, she feared, might take away her daughter. The therapist saw Ms Matthew, her mother, her daughter, and the social services social worker.

After asking questions about the relationship between the social worker and Ms Matthew and the worries each had, the therapist focused on questions to highlight beliefs in the family concerning violence. Ms Matthew's mother had been in a violent relationship with her father but had left him about five years ago. While she was growing up, Ms Matthew had also been hit by him. The therapist asked whether other women in the family had been with violent men, and how people explained this. Ms Matthew and her mother identified a belief that they deserved no better and neither had they believed that there was any alternative. They also highlighted the importance of being in a relationship with a man, that women were nothing without a man—both of which are beliefs that many women hold. The therapist then pursued how it was that Ms Matthew's mother had finally decided to leave her husband and the meaning of this. Neither of the women had really thought about this or talked with each other about it. Ms Matthew has not returned to her partner.

Work in a women's refuge

Women's refuges have been central in providing safety for women and children from men's violence and also in focusing society's attention on domestic violence. However, refuges struggle with the phenomenon that some women return to the violent relationship from which they have fled. Traicoff (1982) believes the secrecy of the refuges, although useful because of the fear of retaliation by angry and violent male partners, may maintain the secrecy of the violent interaction in an unhelpful way and may also keep battered women as a woman's issue, rather than a community one. Unfortunately, workers in women's refuges have not always seen family/systems workers as very helpful to the women and children who reside there.

Case example
"Life beyond the refuge"

Ms Andrew and her four children were referred to a family therapist after one of the children had started a fire at the refuge. Ms A had been subjected to violence by her husband for a number of years and had left him once before but had returned to him. This time she was being rehoused but believed that her husband would still be in control of her life and that she would get drawn back into the abusive relationship. She presented herself as helpless and victimized and as caught between, on the one hand, the powerful support of the refuge staff (who were becoming irritated by her) and, on the other, the powerful presence of her ex-husband. We see this as a common dilemma for women in refuges when they see themselves as needing to be defined by others, rather than as able to define themselves.

The work focused firstly on supporting Ms Andrew and the children to set a boundary around themselves as a family to prepare for their life together outside the refuge, and this resulted in her being more in control of her children. The focus then shifted to an exploration of the constraints that might prevent her from continuing the process of taking charge of her life.

The therapist raised questions about a number of beliefs she might have, in common with other women, and how these might affect her behaviour. These included feeling that she had no self-worth unless she was in a relationship, even an abusive one; how the patterns of an abusive relationship could be familiar ones that had their safe, predictable aspects; how she might feel that a single-parent family was incomplete or illegitimate; how her experience of male–female power differences might affect her relationship with her sons; and how she might feel she had to take care of her ex-husband.

The therapist explored with her how these beliefs might lead to particular kinds of behaviour, such as always drawing her husband in to take over when she had problems with her sons, and how these behaviours might prevent her gaining control over her life. This enabled her to think about the context for her difficulties and created a more neutral exploratory context for looking at reciprocal patterns, accepting responsibility in a non-blaming way, and seeing the possibility that she could negotiate with her husband about his contact with the children.

We have found that addressing the constraints on women in this situation is helpful, because it avoids the risk, inherent in more straightforward encouragement and strengthening approaches, of frustration and sometimes blame on the part of workers if the woman returns to the abusive relationship.

Indeed, using the framework of constraints has also been very helpful in relation to working with men. For some men, the move to accepting others' views as different from their own makes it more difficult to exercise power in ways that they thought were appropriate as men. In this process, highlighting and eliciting gendered premises can be a helpful way forward for both men and women.

We have drawn on the writing of Alan Jenkins (1990), who highlights societal beliefs as constraints on men who are violent and abusive, preventing them from having different, more sensitive and responsible relationships. In this way he engages men to take responsibility for their violence and challenges those beliefs that they or society might use to absolve them from this responsibility. Some of his questions to male abusers have been particularly helpful, and as therapists we interweave these with other ways of challenging beliefs about power and entitlement.

Case example
"What kind of wife do you want to have?"

During work with a couple who had separated because of the husband's violence, but where he wanted the relationship to continue, the therapist asked the husband whether he was a man who wanted his wife to have similar views to himself, or would appreciate a woman who developed her own ideas, even if these might be different to his? This question made the husband pause for a considerable amount of time as he contemplated these two different versions of himself. He really wanted his wife to agree with him, and yet he wanted to see himself as a man who appreciated women having their own ideas. The therapist went on to explore this dilemma and included those ideas about maleness which might be interfering with other ideas about how he wanted to live. It also enabled the woman to contemplate her own dilemmas about whether the relationship could develop or she should stay separate.

One crucial element in work with couples is to ensure that the relationship is safe from violence and that the therapy itself does not endanger this. We often explicitly contract with the man, who is given responsibility to control his violence in the first session, that we need to be convinced he is able to do this before therapy can continue.

Keeping a balance between holding the man responsible for his violence while unravelling some of the other interactional aspects of the relationship can be tricky territory, particularly given some of the beliefs we discussed early. If a man persists in holding the woman responsible, it can be helpful to ask questions such as "If you don't think you are in control of your violence, how do you think you are going to stop?" Sometimes the woman can experience the initial work, if focused mainly on the man's beliefs and behaviour, as neglecting her concerns. We have had several experiences of men withdrawing from therapy after the violence is talked about; if the woman is able to take action to ensure her safety, this is not necessarily a poor outcome. It is more problematic if the woman continues to come and report on what sounds like a highly dangerous situation; again, we try to keep safety to the forefront of the conversation.

It is important to make a distinction for women between being responsible for interactions in the relationship and being responsible for violence. This crucial distinction is easy to blur. In work with one couple, the man was asked to take responsibility for observing when he still had the choice to do something other than becoming violent, and the woman was asked to think about how he experienced her ambivalence, for which she needed to take a different responsibility.

Case example
"Can you afford any anger?"

In work with another couple, where the man had managed to stop his violence before they came to therapy, the couple and the therapist unravelled the other interactions in the family that contributed to beliefs about control and domination that were continuing to make their relationship very uncomfortable. The man decided he had found a solution by never becoming angry but then feeling as if he had let himself down terribly if he did so. The woman interpreted every loss of temper as a sign that the violence was about to restart and reacted powerfully and bitterly. The challenge for this couple was how to find ways to disagree that would stay safe and allow an appreciation of their differences.

THE THERAPIST'S POSITION

We consider, as women therapists, that it is important to understand how societal beliefs shape what happens in the relationship between the couple and the therapist. In work with one couple, a powerful belief was highlighted that the man felt he could not listen to a woman and be influenced by her, because this would contradict his belief that he had to be in control and not be dependent in any way. This placed the therapist in a difficult position. How could he listen to her, as she was a woman?

While we may hold as an ideal that couples work with violence should be carried out by mixed-sex teams, in practice this is often not possible. It then becomes important for therapists and consulting teams to pay attention to how they can join with the viewpoint of the person in the minority. If the man who has been violent is the "odd one out", this may pose particular challenges to female therapists and consultants to join without being either over-blaming or overprotective.

Case example
"Aren't you insulted?"

A couple had been to therapy with a woman therapist, together with a woman colleague consulting in the room, for several sessions with worries about the children before the wife revealed that her husband had raped her on several occasions after social functions where he had had too much to drink. She described how distressed and frightened she had been, and her husband sat looking abject and embarrassed but said that, since he had no recollection of doing this, he did not know what he could do about it. Eventually, they had both been to see their GP, who took the line that wives just had to put up with these things. The therapist found it hard to contain her indignation on the wife's behalf. The consultant said that she felt even more indignant on the husband's behalf and that, if she were he, she would be insulted that the GP had such a low opinion of him that he did not expect him to be responsible for his own actions. Following this session the husband took the initiative in seeking help for himself.

Although a gender imbalance produces its own constraints, we regard this as preferable to working alone with these difficult and emotionally demanding cases, and as particularly valuable when making the tough decision that therapy is likely to be unhelpful or counterproductive.

CHAPTER 6

Stories lived and told: language and discourse

> "They cut off my voice, so I grew two voices, into different tongues my songs I pour."
>
> Alicia Partnoy (1986)

In this chapter we draw on some ideas from feminist linguistics and discourse analysis to examine the relationship between language and experience. We discuss how a narrative approach to therapy has been particularly helpful in affirming women's experiences that have been ignored and denied.

We see therapy as a place where people not only ask for help with a specific problem but where questions about personhood are raised, and negotiations about identities take place, even though these latter agendas are often not explicit. Because new stories can be generated in therapy, issues that have concerned us as therapists are the availability of stories in our culture and the limitations of language.

We find narrative to be a particularly fitting metaphor in therapy. By a narrative approach we mean one where the emphasis is on the stories people tell about themselves and the ways in which different stories can be developed, drawing on social constructionist ideas. As we argued in Chapter 2, however, not all meanings can be changed through therapeutic conversations; there are other constraints on meaning-making. We think it is important to keep in mind that language has real effects, just as meanings are shaped by material conditions and the societal structures in which we live.

LANGUAGE AND GENDER

In thinking about language in therapy, we find it important to see language as a social practice with a history—by which we mean that language is not a neutral tool that can be used to explain or describe our experience but that it fulfills a particular purpose in the organization of our society. Language produces meaning and does not just reflect what we have experienced (Kristeva: see Moi, 1986). It is through language that our gendered lives are "composed".

The work of feminist linguists has aided us in examining aspects of women's relationship to language. One of the most provocative arguments was put by Dale Spender (1980) in her book *Man Made Language*, in which she set out to demonstrate how the English language had encoded a male view that hampered and handicapped women, or, as Daly (1973) described it, women had inherited a "contaminated language". Although Spender had a powerful impact on us in changing our own relationship to language, helping us become observers rather than just users of language, her writing did perpetuate traditional ideas about gender difference (Cameron, 1985). More useful and also more compatible with a systemic approach has been the focus on the struggle over meaning.

Historically, women have been denied access to or rendered silent in those societal institutions—i.e. universities, newspapers, government, and the courts—where the dominant linguistic meanings were developed. Not surprisingly, white middle-class males' experiences and language were also prominent in the building of family therapy theory. Barriers to women continue to operate today, although they have shifted to subtler and more covert means. Such exclusion, not surprisingly, meant that women's experiences and knowledge were either left out or defined from male viewpoints. As Wetherell (1993) wisely points out, if the struggle over meaning is not evident in the construction of social reality, then it is likely that some voices have been silenced. This is not to say that women did not have language or make meanings of their own, but that their talking was marginalized and trivialized by men and by themselves.

One of the tasks both within therapy and outside it has been to reclaim and rework language, to give credence and weight to those ignored or discounted experiences. To counter the neglect of women's writing by the mainstream publishing houses, the Women's Presses were set up in this country by women in the 1970s in the face of considerable opinion that women writers were not significantly talented, nor would there be sufficient demand (Chamberlain, 1988). Their success has been significant and confirmed the importance of bringing to light and validating women's experiences that had been marginalized, neglected, or dismissed. What has been useful is the range and variations of the experiences and dilemmas of women of different races, cultures, and classes. These have challenged some of the universalizing social constructions about womenhood.

These books provide important cultural narratives for women, including ourselves, through which to validate different experiences, thinking, and world visions. We draw on this range of stories indirectly to help think about what is unsaid in our therapy, but also more directly. For example, in our work with women who have been sexually abused, we may recommend books such as *I Know Why the Caged Bird Sings* (Angelou, 1984), or *Cry Hard and Swim* (Spring, 1987), as these public accounts can sometimes counter the secrecy and perceived shame of the experiences.

NARRATIVE APPROACHES

Narrative approaches fit well with thinking about gendered lives. Adapted from the literary field, their main premise is that our speaking is both "produced" by us and "produces" us (or defines us), as we speak. In interaction with others, we construct our stories over and over again, and give meaning to our various experiences. We tell the stories we live, and live the stories we tell. However, "narrative structures organize and give meaning to experience, but there are always feelings and lived experiences not fully encompassed by the dominant story" (E. Bruner, 1986). Many of our experiences remain outside language, although these are also influenced and shaped by language (see Harré, 1986, for a discussion of the social construction of emotions, and hooks, 1989, on the relationship between language, race, and gender).

As we see it, therapeutic dialogue can enable people to discover their stories through the telling. At times, change happens in the telling, as the experience of becoming a subject in our own story fundamentally alters our relationship to events in which we experienced ourselves as passive. At other times, the importance is not in the telling but in the reflecting on and curiosity in the story we have told, which illuminates the impact of that particular form of narrative, that genre, on us. Wilkes (1994) has called this an "ironic" stance, one that is particularly helpful to interrogate the idealized narratives about womanhood.

White and Epston's (1990) re-storying approach—in which they help people recount their "problem-saturated" stories and externalize these, in order to separate themselves from these stories—has provided a useful framework. Their notions of "unique outcomes" and exceptions (i.e. experiences that had not previously been noticed) have been helpful in the development of new stories. Sometimes "externalizing the problem" fits too closely with traditional male constructions of self (see Chapter 3), with phrases like "beating the problem" and "overcoming the problem-saturated story" employing images of will-power and taking charge of oneself which are not always helpful. Sometimes externalizing the problem *is* the problem for men in particular, so that re-storying may need to include new ways of conceptualizing problems. On the other hand, externalizing the problem may be extremely liberating for some women who specialize in internalizing them.

Drawbacks may arise in working with exceptions or "unique outcomes" because they raise dilemmas for clients' loyalty and commitment to old stories. Some people come to therapy with a very strong attachment to their stories, "mentally touching, caressing over and over again the same old thoughts" (Alvarez, 1992) which exclude other ways to think and be.

Case example
"But this has been my life's work"

A woman who was admitted to psychiatric hospital because of severe depression and suicidal behaviour was seen for therapy with her husband. She described how part of the reason for her admission to hospital was her intense frustration that she had been unable to help her husband who suffered from crippling migraine attacks and had an eating disorder, and her feeling that his illnesses were destroying their relationship. The therapist explored a pattern with her of sacrificing her own needs, both in her family of origin and now in this relationship. This was such a powerful story that she saw suicide as a preferable option to leaving the relationship although it had become untenable.

In the following session, she was extremely distressed and talked about how people had been telling her she ought to put herself first more. However, she felt that if she embraced this view, she would be invalidating the entire premise on which she had based her life so far and would not be able to make sense of her life if she did this. Clearly, there was a need for the "old story" to be validated positively before a new story could emerge.

Others consider their lived experience as outside the norm, outside cultural narratives. This is not to imply that experience lies dormant, separate, waiting to be expressed, but that the narratives available to us shape both what we ignore and what we feel we can experience. Therapy can replicate an experience of marginalization if we, too, ignore family members' lived experience (Byrne & McCarthy, 1994), or it may involve the therapist and family members in a search for narratives that can give meanings to experiences previously disowned.

TRAUMA AND STORYING

There are a group of people who have lived experiences of such trauma that, in order to survive, they could not allow themselves to acknowledge these to give them meaning. Without a story these experiences also become disconnected from the person, and the person protected from them. These persons may be caught between preferring silence as a sanctuary, and a wish to bear witness, to give testimony (Felman & Laub, 1992). Because our culture privileges articulate speaking—e.g. public figures are judged on their wit and skill at parrying questions—silence has been considered oppression and often invites definition by others. The French feminists (Irigaray, 1985; Kristeva [Moi, 1986]) have warned of the implications for women of taking on narrative forms with a beginning, middle, and end because these may distort and subvert the fragmentation and multiplicity of experiences (Moi, 1988) which, we have argued, particularly constitute female lived experience. We sometimes view therapy as bearing witness to fragments, ambiguities, and incompleteness, without trying to capture the experiences or go for the closure of coherent narrative.

We are aware of a particular tension in our therapeutic work with women (but also with men who have suffered abuse or trauma) around whether a new narrative can really be co-constructed, or how much we are invited to determine the direction or content of the story. In brief solution-focused work, for example, therapists often take a very fixed view about the *form* the story should take, although the details, the *content*, are left to the client. There seems little place for fragments or ambiguities here.

One important idea we have developed is to pay attention to the sources on which the woman depends in knowing herself (here, Belenky et al.'s 1986 work has helped us think about the relational context of women's knowledge of themselves, and social constructionism about the societal context). Many women who have been through brutalizing experiences or have been overly defined by others, go on to try to find their own voices by blocking out feedback from others. This can create other complications in their relationships, as well as cutting them off from other views that might be helpful to them. In this position it is also difficult for them to get a critical edge on their own thinking, as they are intent on developing and valuing their own knowledge. In these situations we often find it helpful to interest the woman in the process of how she learns about herself over time, as this can give her another view. For example, in work with a woman who came for therapy with her violent husband, she defined herself in an individual session as an addicted personality, addicted to her relationship. When the therapist asked her how and when she had come to see herself in this way, it emerged that this story had been authored by her partner. These questions were unsettling to her ideas both about herself, hence opening other alternatives, but also about the process of how she had come to experience herself.

MULTIPLE AND OVERLAPPING STORIES

Jerome Bruner has said, "culture itself comprises an ambiguous text that is constantly in need of interpretation by those who participate in it" (1986, p. 122), so paying attention to the way language creates social reality is of crucial importance to everyone. One way to do this is through the use of discourse analysis—a focus on the social organization of talk, the ways in which certain themes and topics are generally discussed, which allow certain ways of thinking and undermine and exclude others (Potter & Wetherell, 1987; Wetherell & Potter, 1992).

Discourses about motherhood create stories for women about themselves as mothers. An examination of childcare and parenting manuals using discourse analysis revealed that, although stating that there are many ways to mother, they perpetuated a universalizing story about mothering as "ultimate fulfillment", constant availability, and putting babies' interests first (Marshall, 1991). These cultural stories create tensions when mothers' experiences of parenting contradict these official versions. In therapy, women sometimes explicitly define themselves negatively in relation to this story (Burck & Frosh, 1993), which often remains implicit and unchallenged in therapeutic conversations.

Case example
"Learning to be your own back-up"
Ms Hall, a single-parent mother, requested family therapy with her son Tony, age 6 years, because of his temper tantrums. She had previously been to an individual therapist who suggested it

was her fault. This made her feel terrible, and Tony's difficulties continued. The family therapy sessions enabled Tony's temper tantrums to be viewed in the context of his father's erratic contact and of her transition to becoming a single parent. Ms Hall found it very difficult to believe in her own sense about what would be useful for her son. Her mother gave her lots of advice, which made her feel even more inadequate. When the therapist asked what her mother knew about bringing up a child on her own, she became very thoughtful and said that perhaps she really didn't know, as she had never been a single parent. This in turn made it easier to explore her own ideas and beliefs. When the therapist asked about her ideas on discipline, Ms Hall remembered that her own father had been violent to them as children. Setting her ideas about discipline in this past context moved her from a story about being ineffective, to someone who wanted to develop different ways to be firm with her son. In the next session, she is exploring with the therapist the changes in her relationship with her son.

Ms Hall: Things are getting on well. I've resolved a few things myself, and done a lot of thinking. I think why things have improved, is that I've decided on some things I wanted and stuck by them. Before I was wishy-washy with guidelines for John.

Therapist: How is it that you became clearer for yourself?

Ms Hall: Before that I always felt guilty about stopping him doing things.

Therapist: How did you get to feel less guilty?

Ms Hall: I'm learning to be a Mum.

Therapist: I wonder if because you were a girl, you were brought up expected to listen to others rather than yourself?

Ms Hall: Maybe that was why. When I had no backup, I wasn't sure what was right or wrong.

Therapist: How have you discovered that you can be your own backup?

Ms Hall: Now, I think, this is what I've decided and I can carry it through.

For mothers to be able to re-story themselves, therapists also need to unhook themselves from the dominant story of motherhood. Sometimes we address ideas about responsibility directly in therapy, asking the husband questions such as: "Why is it that your wife describes herself as responsible for your son's problem?" "Do you think this is to do with her being a woman, as women often see themselves as responsible, or more to do with her personally?" "What is the effect of her feeling so responsible? What would have to happen for her not to feel so responsible?" "What if you started to feel more responsible?"

EXPLORING THE CONTRADICTIONS

Unless we ourselves become familiar with the power of discourse, we may not notice what is not being said or asked, or where our own and others' stories are constrained.

Marshall (1986) interviewed a group of women managers about their work, who all agreed that being women did not affect them in their jobs. This was the dominant discourse. When she went on to ask questions about the details of their work tasks and working relationships, different stories emerged, and these women went on to discuss many dilemmas that they faced as women managers (Hollway, 1989). Kaplan's (1992) study of mothers found that most of her subjects engaged in no social critique at all. Although they were unhappy and thought mothers could not win, whether working or not working, they explained this as lack of support from other women, rather than in terms of contradictions inherent in mothering in this society. This is another example of how little we like to think of ourselves as influenced by society, and personalize and individualize our experiences. This, say Wetherell and White (1992), is another sign of the power of discourse. For those of us who strive to make links between family interactions and the societal context, it is an important constraint. In therapy we consider the aim of therapeutic talk as discovering, making available, and being able to draw on multiple discourses to make sense of the many contradictions we live.

Case example
"Two stories, not one"

A woman and her children came into therapy following a terrifying experience of an armed robbery. The father, who had not been present and had been brought up in a war-torn society where he often faced life-and-death situations, insisted they should not be afraid. The mother faced a dilemma between validating the children's and her own experience and the way this was being defined for them. For the mother this was crucial, as her childhood experience of sexual abuse meant she had had to accept others' definitions and discredit her own. Therapy enabled her to validate her own experience and story, as well as gain an understanding of what her husband's view entailed. In exploring his belief, it emerged that he saw showing no fear as the only way in which he had managed to escape death in his country of origin. This enabled the mother to develop a view of two alternative stories, neither of which cancelled out the other.

DIFFERENT DISCURSIVE STYLES

One of us [CB] recently set up a small research project with a colleague to examine how men and women presented themselves in family therapy,[1] and found that women and men often used different discursive styles, particularly when there was marked disagreement between them over how the problem was seen. We see these not as essentialist gender differences, but as traditional ways of gaining credence (Edwards & Potter, 1992). Men more generally drew on a scientific style, producing facts that spoke for themselves, which concealed them as observers and put a distance between them and the problem (a form of presentation useful in work settings). Women often used a story-telling style, presenting rich contextual and relational detail which included themselves in the account and invited validation because it implied direct experience.

Because women counted themselves into the story as interpreters and observers, issues of emotional responsibility are embedded in these descriptions. This discursive style can be viewed as reflecting but also as "producing" women's responsibilities for family problems. For men, the distance from the problem, and the invitation to others to discuss at the level of accepted knowledge, excludes any idea of personal responsibility or of self-interest in this view. However, adopting this more problem- and solution-oriented view may lead men to take responsibility for carrying out tasks.

In becoming more aware of discursive style, we are interested in how the context of therapy can allow different descriptions to emerge. Anything that can help people reflect on language itself and question meanings can have an impact on their relation to themselves and to their stories. Cooper (1990) has worked with women to enable them to become observers to discursive style in their work settings, which has allowed an experimentation both in the therapy and at work with locating themselves within different discourses. To change one's use of language means that one is no longer just shaped by it. This is one aspect of the importance of asking people to keep diaries in therapy, particularly in work with sexual abuse, where it has been especially important to gain distance, clarity, and control over the experiences. (See Gorell Barnes & Henessy, 1994, for one moving account, by a therapist and client, of the use of a diary in therapy.)

In the context of therapy, women may seek affirmation through facilitating a connection with the therapist, being mindful of the power imbalance. We have a hypothesis that women sometimes define themselves as needing help in therapy as a way to do this. Men, on the other hand, may use language to explore the rules and hierarchy of therapy and be more preoccupied with power and decision-making as the route to being validated. This focus can act as a constraint on evolving a reflexive narrative of self, which Giddens (1992) has argued men urgently need to develop. When men viewed their own experiences as the norm, there was no need to become self-reflexive.

Case example
"Making decisions or looking after"

A couple came to therapy for help following the death of their child. At one point in the therapy the couple were discussing whether or not they would have more children in the future.

John: I will never ever be able to have another child. I just don't think I would be able to go through that experience again.

Anne (*upset, because she very much wants to have another baby*): Even if I thought something like that, if I knew that he wanted something different, I would not say it, because I would know it would hurt him.

This excerpt demonstrates the very different meanings communication sometimes has for men and women. Here a woman sees her communication as a means of looking after the relationship, while the man sees stating his view as important in order to make decisions.

The interactive patterns that develop between women and men can sometimes be seen as a battle about discursive style rather than meaning. Sometimes we have had the experience in therapy of women repeating their stories endlessly, which their partners and sometimes therapists interrupt, so that these women's struggle for some kind of recognition for themselves and their story becomes disqualified through the process which leads to further repetition. Where others would experience this story-telling as redundant information, these repetitions can also be seen a persistence in the struggle for the survival of their experience.

We see therapy as enabling family members to have access to a number of multiple and alternative discourses or cultural stories with which to discuss their experiences and life events. To move from one dominant discourse to various alternatives allows hidden or ignored experiences to be affirmed and owned and richer, more complex stories to be lived. However, although we stay hopeful about the transformative possibilities of words, we do not always put words and stories as the most important context in the face of such powerful narrative-shaping circumstances as poverty, racism, and war. Therapy is not enough.

NOTE

1. This research project into gender narratives in family therapy was set up with Stephen Frosh and is being conducted at the Tavistock Clinic (Burck & Frosh, 1993; Burck & Frosh, submitted).

CHAPTER 7

Case studies

The two cases presented here demonstrate in more detail the way we apply the ideas explored in this book in our therapeutic work. Although we have chosen sections that highlight how we work with issues around gender, it is important to point out that in neither case did this constitute the whole emphasis of the work.

THERAPEUTIC APPROACH

As already described in the Introduction, our therapeutic approach, influenced by social constructionist ideas, involves a focus on the way family and individual beliefs and meanings have evolved over time and how these connect to current impasses. We address gender in therapy at the levels of the subjective, the relational, and the societal, paying particular attention to the gender premises that individuals hold and that are revealed in their relationships with each other and in their families of origin. A historical perspective is important to us in therapy because it helps us and our clients understand and challenge the contexts in which particular beliefs come about. We try to stay aware of how gender constructions are brought forth or are challenged in our therapeutic conversations.

Within this overall framework, our actual therapeutic method involves asking questions that can generally be defined as reflexive (Tomm, 1987; Campbell, Draper, & Huffington, 1991) and are used to create new contexts for thinking about familiar patterns and stories. Questions sometimes invite family members to become curious about hitherto unexamined assumptions, and at other times to challenge or intensify beliefs. Our experience is that making links to gender premises and societal constraints can allow alternative views to develop that enable both women and men to take appropriate responsibility in a non-blaming way and develop less constraining relationships.

We often use reflecting team conversations (Andersen, 1987), either with a consultant in the room or with the team behind the screen. More idiosyncratically, we will each have different ways of using humour, irony, and metaphor and of setting tasks.

MEN AT THE MARGINS: A MOTHER/DAUGHTER RELATIONSHIP

In this work we explored the hopes and disappointments of a mother/ daughter relationship in the context of a family where men were experienced as absent, violent, or unreliable over three generations. The effect of this on women's expectations of each other, on their own sense of power and of the power of men, was one main focus of the therapy.

The therapist was Gwyn Daniel, and Kirsten Blow (Co-Director, Oxford Family Institute) consulted in the room. The therapist and consultant used reflecting conversations throughout the sessions to expand, amplify, question, and develop the family's and their own beliefs and hypotheses.

Referral

Jacky Ryan telephoned to ask for therapy because of difficulties in her relationship with her daughter, Brenda. Jacky said that they had a very difficult past, with her partner, Mick, being violent towards her and her children. Brenda had made a number of

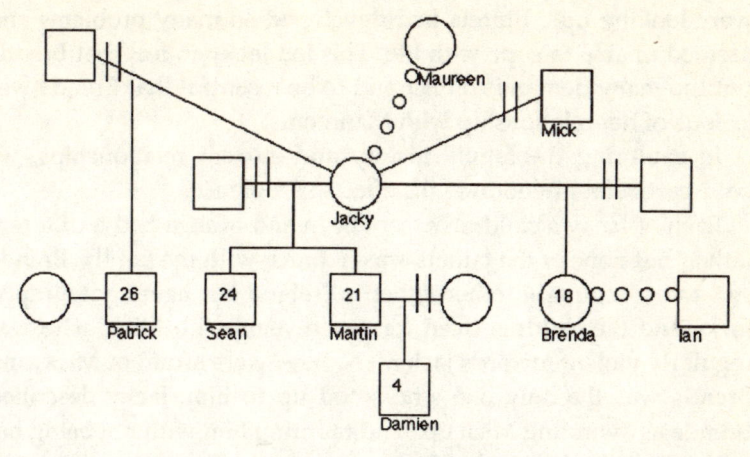

FIGURE 1. Genogram

suicide attempts and had been in an adolescent unit. Jacky said that they had never been able to communicate and that she was very worried about Brenda's current lifestyle.

The family consists of Jacky, a teacher, aged 44, and her four children, Patrick, aged 26, Sean, aged 24, Martin, aged 21, and Brenda, aged 18, who works in a hospital canteen (see Figure 1). Patrick is married with no children, Sean is single, and Martin is a single parent with a 4-year-old son, Damien. Jacky lives with her partner, Maureen, and Brenda lives with her partner, Ian. Jacky's request was for some sessions for herself and Brenda. She did not want to include her sons at this stage.

Session 1

When we asked about the current issues, we learnt from Brenda that what she wanted was a "proper" mother/daughter relationship. She found Jacky's relationship with Maureen embarrassing and felt that her mother never had time for her. She was frightened to talk to her mother because it "always ends in rows". She felt she had never had a childhood because she had to defend her mother when there was violence. We learnt from Jacky that she had struggled hard to free herself from her violent relationship, which involved starting a career, making links with other women, and going into counselling. She was disappointed that, just as "things were looking up", Brenda had developed so many problems and seemed unable to cope with life. This led Jacky to feel that Brenda put too many demands on her and to be resentful that Brenda was jealous of her relationship with Maureen.

In exploring the family history and current relationships, we paid particular attention to the effects of violence.

Each of Jacky's children except Sean and Martin had a different father, but none of the fathers was in touch with the family. Brenda still wrote regularly to her father in Ireland but never got a reply. Jacky and the children lived for seven years with Mick, who was regularly violent towards Jacky. The boys were afraid of Mick, and Brenda was the only one who stood up to him. Jacky described Brenda as "winding Mick up" and taunting him with not being her father. She tried to stop her for her own safety. Brenda's recollection was of Mick separating her and Jacky so that they could not be close. When the therapist explored their explanations for why Jacky stayed with Mick, we learnt that Jacky felt she did not have a mind of her own when she was with Mick. Brenda wavered between understanding her mother's position of not being able to support herself and her children away from Mick and resentment that Jacky gave in too much to him. They were able to identify a pattern where Jacky gave in to Mick to protect the children and Brenda stood up to Mick in the way she thought her mother should.

We learnt that in the family now, the eldest son, Patrick, is married and settled and seen as being very responsible. He supports Jacky when she and Brenda have rows by being very critical and blaming of Brenda. The second son, Sean, is frequently depressed and has difficulty holding down a job. The youngest son, Martin, looks after his son on his own, with a great deal of help from Jacky. Brenda had made two suicide attempts around the time Jacky was leaving Mick and setting up on her own; she had disappeared from home for several weeks and lived in London. During this time, she became pregnant with twins and had a miscarriage. Jacky was unable to be with her because an aunt to whom she was close was dying. Brenda had had a second miscarriage four months before the first interview.

At present Jacky's worries about Brenda revolved around her drinking, her inability to keep a job, her mismanaging money, and the fact that she lied to cover up mistakes. Jacky believed it was important for Brenda to be independent and strong and that her current difficulties were due to lack of self-esteem. Brenda retorted that she needed her mother, she had to book an appointment to see her, and that she was owed some time with her now.

The therapeutic aim at the end of this session was to connect Brenda and Jacky in a positive way and to link their current dilemmas with past experiences in order to give them a new view.

The therapist took up the theme of independence and positively connoted Jacky's wish for Brenda to be strong so that she would not go through the same experiences as her mother. However, the therapist also raised the question of how Brenda understood this message. When Jacky encouraged her to be "more independent", Brenda might feel she was being pushed away. The therapist thought Brenda had been very strong to stand up to Mick as she did, but perhaps this was hard for Jacky to acknowledge because it made her feel guilty. Perhaps, also, Brenda had understood that, in order to be more separate, you first needed to feel more connected.

Session 2

At the beginning of this session, there was a more positive atmosphere between Jacky and Brenda. They had more contact and had shared worries about Patrick, the eldest brother, who had been in hospital.

The therapist asked Brenda what sort of a daughter she thought Jacky expected her to be. Brenda said she thought it was to be like Patrick, who is the perfect brother—reliable and supportive. Jacky was very surprised by this answer and when asked how she would have answered the question, said that she would want Brenda to be a daughter who could do things for herself and be independent.

> Therapist (*interested in the value given to independence and concerned to "unpack" it a bit*): Can you tell me how she would be if she was independent?
>
> Jacky: She would do things for herself and not rely on anyone else.

The therapist asked Brenda when she thought she had come nearest to Jacky's ideal for her. Brenda talked about the time when she was alone in hospital having a miscarriage and did not ask Jacky to come and look after her; this was a painful story, but Brenda seemed to take it for granted that Jacky's aunt should take precedence.

The therapist and consultant had a reflecting conversation about this story, saying that they thought this represented the ultimate in Brenda showing independence and speculated about the advantages and disadvantages of giving up your own needs in this way. Had Brenda learnt well from Jacky about how you were valued as a woman if you always put others before yourself?

The therapist then asked about Jacky's family background. She was brought up in Ireland, one of two daughters. Jacky did not know her father, whom her mother never married. Jacky's grandmother lived with them and was unwell, needing her mother to take care of her. When Jacky was 17, she left home and became pregnant; she kept the baby (Patrick) despite family opposition.

At the end of the session, the therapist and consultant reflected on their understanding of the intergenerational patterns. They discussed how daughters looked after mothers and that this was particularly important in the absence of reliable men. Thus a rule seemed to have developed in the family that daughters needed to be independent so that mothers could be free to attend to the generation above. This had been the case for Jacky with her mother and grandmother, and Brenda had perhaps been loyal to this pattern when she allowed her mother to attend to her aunt rather than to her. We were interested in whether Brenda, by demanding more of her mother, was now challenging this rule and whether, by not taking Jacky's advice, she was also trying to show how independent she was.

Session 3

In this session, where there was again an atmosphere of mutual blame, Jacky described criminal activities Brenda had been involved in, in the past, which she feared were still continuing. She wanted an explanation for why Brenda had done this.

The therapist asked each what their most feared explanation for Brenda's behaviour was. Brenda said that it would mean she was "just a bad lot", Jacky that it would mean *she* had done something wrong. Brenda then more directly criticized her mother for lack of attention and again expressed her view that Mick had deliberately split them. Jacky said that it was Brenda's behaviour that split them and that she and Mick agreed on discipline. She described how when Brenda was at the height of her activities, the police were always at the house; they were almost part of the family.

In a reflecting conversation with the consultant, the therapist said how struck she was by this picture. It was as if there were two kinds of crime going on: public crimes in which Brenda was involved, and private crimes in which Mick was involved. Perhaps bringing the police in was Brenda's way of trying to protect her mother? We could see Jacky was finding this difficult to hear because she was feeling blamed, and we wondered how important it was for her to minimize the effect of the violence on her relationship with Brenda.

Exploring the theme of guilt led to a discussion of how Brenda felt she could never be good enough for her mother, unlike the boys. "Were they perfect", asked the therapist, "because of their characters, or because of their sex?"

The therapist and consultant speculated about why Jacky and Brenda had to be so perfect for each other and connected this to their difficulty in validating each other's story about the violence. We were interested that disappointment in each other had a different intensity from disappointment in sons and brothers.

Validating each of their stories had a powerful effect on Jacky and Brenda in this session.

Session 4

In the fourth session, there appeared to be a dramatic change in the relationship between Jacky and Brenda, with a level of warmth and togetherness we had not seen before. Interestingly, this accompanied another crisis for Jacky, who was worried about her second son, Sean, who had disappeared with a disreputable friend.

Much of the discussion in this session was around the belief that men were more vulnerable than women and that women could be held more responsible for their actions.

We explored Jacky's belief that Sean's depression was attributable to the violence in a way that she did not think Brenda's difficulties were. In addition to this, Brenda and Jacky were also able to see their anger with each other as part of the belief that women could be expected to take more than men could. At the end of this session, Brenda voiced for the first time her fears that her partner, Ian, would be violent to her, and she described some worrying incidents.

Session 5

The following transcript is from the fifth session, when Jacky and Brenda were continuing to report an improvement in their relationship, which again centred around worries about the brothers. The therapist wondered if being engaged in joint caretaking was what brought them close.

>Therapist: So when you have worries about the boys, what does that do to the relationship between the two of you?
>
>Jacky: I quite often ring Brenda to talk to her. It's like I'm happier talking to her.
>
>Therapist: What effect do you think that has on Brenda?
>
>Jacky (*taking this as a criticism and answering defensively*): I don't know, I've never thought about it.
>
>Therapist: Do you think Brenda feels more valued by you when you do that?
>
>Jacky: Maybe she does. But I feel maybe I unload all my problems onto her.
>
>Therapist: Is that a balance, then, that you struggle with? How to share things with Brenda without putting too much on to her?
>
>Jacky: I think when things like that come up it feels like she's a colleague, rather than a daughter; she's somebody else I can talk to about how I feel. She understands a lot. It's valuable.
>
>Therapist: She has a lot of wisdom?
>
>Jacky: I think she's a lot of common sense. I don't always agree, but I always value what she has to say.

Therapist: How do you think she has acquired this wisdom/common sense?

Jacky: I suppose it's got to do with the way the women in our family have always been the strong ones. Maybe that's why it's harder for me when she isn't. I assume that because she's a woman in the family she's going to be someone I can get support from.

Consultant (*to therapist*): What would have to happen for Jacky and Brenda to do that with Brenda as a daughter? I'm not sure why she has to be a colleague.

Jacky (*long pause*): I don't know really. I think I treat her the same as my mother treated me.

Therapist: So would you have felt closer to your mother when you were being a colleague or a support?

Jacky: I didn't have a good relationship with my mother in my teens. A rebel right the way through until I was 18 and had my first child.

Therapist: So if you had gone to your mother wanting her help as a daughter, how would that have affected the relationship?

Jacky: I didn't do that until after I was a mother.

Therapist (*to Brenda*): You've been listening to this, Brenda. I wonder how you think about it. I remember when you first came you said you wanted an ordinary mother–daughter relationship.

Brenda: I suppose now we've been much closer. She doesn't talk down to me, she talks to me like an adult. She sees me as responsible to look after Damien [her nephew]. It's like I'm an adult now. We haven't had a fight for a while now. I've sorted all my money out. She talks to me on a level. But she does help me. I've not done any stupid things. Her whole attitude to me has changed.

The therapist is still preoccupied with the idea that Jacky and Brenda get close when there is looking after others to be done.

Therapist: I was wondering, just suppose there were no big worries about your brothers, how do you think that would affect your relationship?

Brenda: I don't think it would make any difference. Once we've got this far. I don't think it will change now.

Therapist (*persisting*): What I was also wondering was whether you feel especially close when you are both engaged in some joint caring?

Brenda (*struggling a bit*): I don't think just because we weren't caring for the boys she wouldn't do things, it's just when looking after Damien and that she needs more of a family there sort of thing.

The therapist and the consultant explore the possibilities for Jacky and Brenda to get together without necessarily having to be looking after anyone.

(*Jacky raises the question of her relationship with Maureen and Brenda's difficulty with it.*)

Therapist (*to Brenda*): If your Mum had been in a relationship with a man, how do you think that would have been different? Would you have been feeling as left out?

Brenda: I don't honestly think it would have made any difference. But if she'd been with a fella, I think I'd be worrying, is he going to hit her? I think she's better off with Maureen. I don't think she'd be happy if she was with a guy like Mick.

Therapist: Yes, I can see Jacky's happier with Maureen. I suppose I was also wondering about women being expected to be so strong in your family, and whether, if Jacky was with a man, you two would be the only two women in the family and whether you'd feel you'd have more of a place?

Brenda: No I don't think so. In the beginning I used to compete for Mum's attention. When she was with Mick, I did too, but now Maureen doesn't stop me talking with Mum. With Mick it was always, "You've got to be off the phone." "Gotta do this, gotta do that." Now with Maureen it's easier. Some things I can't tell Mum, I can tell Maureen. She'll support me. It works both ways. (*She talks about how much her mother has changed since being with Maureen.*)

The therapist has been holding in mind Brenda's statement in the previous session about violence from her partner.

>Therapist: When you said that if Jacky had been in a relationship with a man you'd have been worried, do you think Jacky worries about you, in your relationship?
>
>Brenda: Yes, I know she worries when me and Ian get into arguments. When we have arguments I always phone her, yes, she does worry.
>
>Therapist: Is that something the two of you have been able to talk about?
>
>Jacky: Yes, I think so, I think I've said that I worry about her. Sometimes I find it difficult to know whether I support her in the way she wants me to. Last Monday she phoned and said she wanted to come home and I didn't encourage her and afterwards I worried that I removed somewhere for her to go to.
>
>Therapist: When you think about that, what do you think you get caught up in?
>
>Jacky: I think about what was happening to me and I find it hard to think about what is the right thing for Brenda because I react with the feeling I would have had.
>
>Therapist: If you just reacted from the gut when Brenda phoned you up, what would that reaction lead you to do?
>
>Jacky: Of course I would say, "You can come home any time you want to".
>
>Therapist: Would that reaction be, "Oh, she's being beaten up"?
>
>Jacky: Yes.
>
>Brenda (*interrupting*): She has actually said that to me once and I said no but she does worry. But when me and Ian fight, it's when he's been drinking and he does turn really nasty when he's been drinking, but I nag him, so it's a vicious circle. He's

got a stomach ulcer and shouldn't drink and I tell him not to and he goes out and gets drunk or brings some home.

Therapist (*to Jacky*): When you hear Brenda speak about this, is there anything in the way she talks about her part in it that triggers off memories for you?

Jacky: Not really ... (*indistinct*): Mick didn't drink like that.

Therapist: I was wondering, and I don't know if this makes sense to you, whether you thought there was anything about Brenda taking responsibility that was familiar to you?

Jacky: Oh, like taking the blame, do you mean? Oh, yes.

Therapist: How do you explain that Brenda might do that?

Jacky (*sadly*): Well, as she grew up seeing me do that, it's not surprising that she does it, that it's difficult for her to say, well, he's an adult, he's got to be responsible.

The therapist is trying to create an opening for Jacky to feel she can offer Brenda something.

Therapist: So is it difficult to say that to Brenda? Or does taking the blame yourself for the past handicap you?

Jacky: I don't think it stops me *saying* it to Brenda. But at the same time I know it's what I used to do. I know it's not easy to get away from doing it.

Therapist: Do you think there is anything Brenda could learn from your experience that would help her?

Jacky: Well, I think there's something about always taking responsibility instead of them being responsible that doesn't help things at all. But it's scary because when you think that then it means you've got to do something about it. When you think about who you are and that you are your own person, then you have to do something and that meant leaving. Or you push the responsibility back to them which means they've got to do something. It doesn't necessarily mean the relationship's got to end, just that it's got to be different.

The therapist explores with Jacky the possible anxiety for Brenda about pushing things that far and risking losing the relationship.

Therapist (*to Brenda*): I wonder what you have been making of what Jacky's been talking about?

Brenda: Well, I can see what she's been saying, but I've done my best to stop him drinking. He only drinks cider now, but I know why he's drinking. (*She talks about all the pressure Ian has at work and worries about his health.*) So I can understand, know what I mean . . . but I wouldn't leave him because of his drinking.

Therapist: What would you leave him for?

Brenda: The only thing that would make me leave him would be if he once laid a hand on me or, if we had kids, on the kids. I can put up with his insecurity or his jealousy and checking up on me, but if he laid a hand on me.

Here, the therapist decides not to continue to challenge Brenda's making little of the effect of her partner's threatening behaviour. She is aware that taking care of Ian is a source of self-esteem to Brenda. She decides to look for a story that will validate Brenda's ability to make a decision to look after herself.

Therapist: I remember from our first session that you said that you had been in a violent relationship before and that you had left it.

Brenda: Er, I can't think now . . . (*struggles*). Mum, help me . . . (*laughs*) Oh, you must mean Gary.

The therapist expresses astonishment that she can't remember.

Brenda: Well, it was a long time ago. He was either on drugs, in prison, or on a high from stealing cars. He was the only one that really laid a hand on me.

Therapist: So what was it, Brenda, that made you decide you weren't going to put up with it any longer?

(*Brenda describes all the delinquent activities this boyfriend got into and drew her into.*)

The therapist persists with the question.

Brenda: Well, it was that he was lying to me. He was promising to give up cannabis and other drugs and to give up stealing cars. The next thing I knew, he'd been nicked.

Therapist (*taking a more ironic and playful stance*): If you wanted to be a rescuer or a caretaker, he could have provided you with material for the rest of your life! Perhaps you should have stuck with him.

Brenda (*laughs*): Yes but he didn't have respect for me, know what I mean. (*She describes all the trouble she got into, e.g. truancy, running away from home.*)

Therapist: You know, we each have a story about our lives. I'm interested in the story of Brenda. Jacky has talked about how she has learnt to look at herself in a different way. Do you think you can spot a time when you thought about yourself in a different way, so it wasn't just what Gary was doing or what Jacky or Mick were doing but what you did differently?

(*Brenda continues to talk about Gary.*)

Therapist: So you could have stuck with it or gone nicking cars with him.

Brenda: I wasn't any good at it. I'd have got caught or gone on to drugs or kept running away. (*She describes a friend telling her to take herself and her life seriously and how she decided to listen to her.*)

Therapist: So a friend triggered off the thought, "Maybe I am worth more than that?"

Brenda: Yes.

The therapist and consultant have a reflecting conversation where they discuss the issue of women feeling that they need to rescue men. The consultant raises a question of Brenda deciding on a boyfriend who would really annoy Mick. This may have diverted Mick's attention from Jacky. Perhaps by doing that Brenda was trying to save Jacky. We discussed what men can be for women, and our confusion about what women could be for each other in this family. If women were close, would they be seen as too powerful? Women spend so much time rescuing men that there is no time to nurture each other. If you have daughters, is there an expectation that they should be nurturing you? Is there an idea that there is only so much nurturing, and it all goes out to men? There must be an expectation that girls don't need so much. If they demand it, it's seen as unreasonable.

> Therapist (*to Jacky and Brenda*): As you can see, these are some of the ideas we are struggling with. What ideas do you have from listening?
>
> Jacky: Yes. There is a difficulty in the family in that . . . my grandmother grew up without a mother; her mother died. Her husband, he wasn't very well, so she had to be quite strong. Then my mother, she looked after her mother and she had to be strong.
>
> Therapist: What about your father?
>
> Jacky: My mother never married my father. She brought us up on her own.

The therapist explores the question of women bringing children up on their own. What do they expect of each other? What do they expect of men? How do they know what to expect of men if there isn't any experience of a close positive relationship with a man? The therapist asks Brenda about her expectations of her own father.

> Brenda: I wrote to him for a long time, but he never bothered to write back, so I thought, "What's the point?" I've given up writing now.
>
> Therapist: That must have been a hard decision for you to take.
>
> Brenda: Not really. If he'd wanted to see me, he could. (*She talks about how she held on to the hope that he wasn't getting her letters and that he was trying to contact her.*) Now I think his family's keeping the letters from him. Either that or he's chucking them in the bin. I'm not kidding myself any more.

The therapist talks about the dilemma about whether to think of him as responsible and give up hope or blame others and keep hopeful about him.

Brenda: He could always find a way if he wanted to (*sadly*).

Therapist: That's holding him responsible.

Brenda: Yes. He's a responsible adult. He's grown up. No reason why he can't pick up a pen and send a postcard or something.

Therapist: Holding him responsible is more realistic, but it means facing your disappointment.

Therapist (*to Jacky*): What advice do you give Brenda about it, because you faced this?

Jacky: Not expecting too much but not assuming that she isn't cared about at all.

Therapist: What ideas about men as partners do you think Brenda has got from her experience?

Jacky: Well, from the men in my life, she wouldn't have learnt that they were particularly reliable or strong people. Rather negative really. He (*talking about Mick*) was extremely jealous, he was jealous of all the children.

The therapist asks about their idea about whether men have to be pandered to if they are to be kept.

Brenda: Most men get jealous in my opinion. Haven't met one that doesn't.

Therapist: So you're pretty cynical then?

Brenda: Yes.

The consultant raises the question of what Jacky is trying to do differently with her sons.

(*Jacky and Brenda both laugh.*)

Jacky: I think Patrick's reliable, but he's got a very strong person in his wife. She very firmly holds the reins.

(*They both discuss how the boys have settled down.*)

The therapist and consultant have a jokey conversation about how Jacky and Brenda sound like two parents discussing a lot of toddlers. The use of humour here allows assumptions to be highlighted and brought into question in a light-hearted way.

> Brenda: That's it, they're babies, all of them.
>
> Therapist: Do you feel more comfortable with them when you think of them as moody and a bit pathetic?
>
> Jacky and Brenda: Yes (*both laugh*).

At the end of the session, the therapist and the consultant discuss the intergenerational pattern of unreliable men and how that affects relationships between women. If there are no models of nurturing or caretaking men, women have to be more there for each other. This is a source of great strength and support but perhaps at the same time something to be feared. The fears might be that it would exclude men altogether, and we could see how that could feed the idea that men are vulnerable, need to be taken care of, and can't be expected to be responsible or behave like adults. We could see this was a bind for Jacky with her sons. Can she take the risk of expecting more of them? We could see a similar bind for Brenda in her relationship with Ian. Would she lose him if she expected him to be responsible for his behaviour?

We also speculated about the effect of Jacky being in a relationship with another woman and whether this would offer an opportunity for Brenda and Jacky to be close without fearing that they will be too close. If Jacky has a rewarding partnership with another woman, she and Brenda might be able to have a mother–daughter relationship that does not have to fulfill everything.

Session 6

In the sixth session, which was also attended by Maureen, we learnt that Brenda had decided to leave Ian after a violent row. She had enlisted Maureen's help in moving out and finding alternative accomodation. Both Jacky and Maureen talked with great pride about how well Brenda had managed this. Brenda also described all the new moves she was making in her life, which included taking GCSEs, attending to her long-standing health problems, and having some individual counselling.

* * *

During this therapy, by inviting mother and daughter to explore their relationship within the context of beliefs and expectations of women of each other over generations, some of the hurts and disappointments of the past could be discussed in a non-blaming way and the process of blaming itself could be challenged and understood differently.

THE MAN AT THE CENTRE OF HIS FAMILY

In this work, we explored the experiences of extreme constraint for all family members in a rigidified gendered pattern of a man struggling with a hazardous life-event and preoccupied with maintaining a sense of self on which he could rely and a woman offering support and recognition without asking for it in return.

Charlotte Burck was the therapist, and John Byng Hall and Barbara Dale (senior staff at the Tavistock Clinic) were the team behind the screen. The team used reflecting conversations with each other behind the screen from which the therapist took ideas that seemed useful. In one session, the therapist and family observed the team's discussion through the screen.

Referral

This family was referred by their GP because their 11-year-old daughter, an only child, had developed ritualistic behaviour which was hampering her everyday life. The GP also mentioned that the father had Crohn's disease, a chronic life-threatening illness, which was exacerbated by stress.

As the therapy with this family continued for a period of almost two years, a few of the main themes in the work have been selected.

First sessions—family work

The first sessions involved the whole family—David, Judy, and Rachel their daughter—and opened up discussions both about Rachel's use of rituals and about the father's illness. It emerged that David also used rituals whose purpose, he said, was to ward off his becoming ill again, and that he was worried both that this meant he was odd or even mad and that he had somehow contaminated Rachel and passed these on to her. However, after acknowledging his ritual use, David, in a rather threatening manner, refused to talk about it.

The therapist decided to take up the theme of "not speaking" as she quickly found that not only the family but also the therapy was very constrained by things that could not be talked about.

Neither Judy nor Rachel pursued conversations that David signalled that he did not want. Rachel talked of being frightened that her father would shout at her were she to discuss any of her concerns with him. When the therapist explored this injunction further, David identified a belief that it was very risky to talk: if you talked about negative things, it would make them happen; if you talked about things getting better, you were tempting fate and things would get worse. Although primarily David's belief, the whole family had organized itself to be very careful of what and how they talked about their situation—it was as if they had developed a type of family ritual to ward off harm. The therapist, who often used hypothetical and future questions with families to explore alternative perspectives of current situations, found that these kinds of questions only reinforced the atmosphere of risk and gloom and were too discrepant with the family's belief. The therapist reflected to the family that, in the context of David's illness, the whole family seemed to be participating in a "ritual of sadness and sorrow" as a way to protect themselves from future disappointment or loss.

In the sessions that followed, the therapist explored with the family the advantages and disadvantages of rituals. In this way we could have a conversation about rituals without needing further clarification about their content, and at the same time, by focusing on the dilemmas of ritual use, this took it out of the realm of "madness" or the fear of madness. We discovered that Rachel's rituals that involved her mother's participation at the point when either she or her mother was leaving the house to go out had begun just at the time when Judy was starting to do more outside the family, something that David openly stated that he did not like. Rachel also said she was very worried that her parents were about to get a divorce because of their arguments.

It is interesting that it was Rachel at age 11 who had asked for help with her "worrying" and had precipitated her family coming to therapy. This is an age when Brown and Gilligan (1992) hypothesize that girls are still willing and able to describe their experiences of relationships from their point of view without becoming too constrained by the impact this has on others (as they do later, particularly in relation to messages about how women should behave). In this family where talking is very restricted, Rachel develops rituals, which puts her father's rituals on the agenda for what seems the first time in this family, and also brings to light her mother's increasing dissatisfaction with the constraints on her developing interests.

Rachel transfers successfully to secondary school and drops many if not most of her rituals. When the therapist explores the family's explanations for how this change has come about, what becomes clear is not only that no one thought they had contributed to this improvement, but that none of them believe that anything they do has an impact on the others. It emerges that this belief protects both mother and daughter from their fears that they could affect the course of David's illness, particularly as it is stress-related. It also keeps David at a distance from fears that his angry and tyrannical behaviour could have an effect on his wife and daughter.

David continues to be silent and withdrawn at times in the family and in the sessions. When the therapist begins to explore this as part of the parental interaction, Rachel intervenes to say that it is her father who is angry nearly all the time. Judy explains this in terms of his physical illness, which causes his depression and his silences and sets the tone for the whole family. In the sessions, David often closes his eyes, saying he wants to go to sleep, leaving Judy both holding the responsibility for the session and treading on eggshells. This theme of Judy taking responsibility and looking after David emerges as a central motif of the parents' relationship, and the therapist keeps this in mind to explore further.

While Rachel continues to express concern about her parents' arguments and her father's anger, both of them say she misunderstands the situation. Although David and Judy disagree with Rachel's view of them, they are concerned about the effect of their relationship on her. The therapist asks what would need to happen for Rachel to be convinced that things were alright in the family. The parents decide that they would like to come to therapy without her, which pleases Rachel; the remaining work is carried out with the parents alone.

Parental/couple work:
Looking after—being looked after

In the next sessions, the premise explored was that, because of his illness, David's experiences were given a central place in the family, with Judy looking after him physically and emotionally. The therapist decided to "unpack" this central premise further, exploring this in the context of the history of their relationship as well as in the context of societal gendered beliefs.

Judy explains that it was David's illness and neediness which had attracted her to him, knowing that if she looked after him he would never leave her. This relationship had solved her concern when she left university that she didn't have any identity. "I could have been persuaded to be almost anyone." As this idea that she had accepted and allowed David and this relationship to define her became more explicit, David began to grow concerned about the implications of her reflections on this. Judy's concern to look after David links both to a societal premise about women's responsibility to care for others and make their needs their own, as well as the premise of the central importance of relationship to women at the cost of other experiences of self.

David's illness, which had entailed many experiences of powerlessness and humiliation through his hospital admissions, his operations, and near death, emphasized his determination to maintain a sense of self on which he could rely, and he counted on his wife to support him in doing so. This position made it very difficult for him to develop different perspectives or for Judy to challenge him. It was as if Judy had become an extension of himself. As Judy's beliefs about herself and their relationship became highlighted in a different way, he became afraid that she might choose to become someone different. He talked about how much he appreciated Judy, and that they had "both realized however bad it is to be together, it is much worse to be on your own.... Being on my own would drive me mad." Here David reveals a fear that a change in Judy would change the basis of their close and special relationship and that he might not survive this.

The belief about madness

David now began to discuss his depression as a major problem which he said often made him worry that he might be "sick in the head" or a "bit mad". In talking about this fear of madness the couple and the therapist move into a different relationship to it. The story about David's "madness" was very powerful and fitted with Judy's experience in her family of origin, as her mother had had several serious breakdowns and had been hospitalized during her growing up. In a sense Judy knew how to live with this, and this "living with" did not question the belief itself. David, who described being very remorseful about his behaviour, at times believed that he could not really be responsible for himself.

Although the therapist herself sometimes felt drawn by the power of the couple's belief, and sometimes felt herself "treading on eggshells", both she and her team noticed that David moved easily from being withdrawn to being engaged and engaging and from being threatening to being cooperative in the sessions. The therapist decided to explore "madness" as a belief that the whole family had acquired about David.

She asks how he had come to think of himself in this way. Through this discussion, the fixedness of "depression" comes into question, and the phrases "acting as if mad" and "demonstrating unusualness" come to take its place, and lead to David talking about himself in different contexts.

> David: What I was going to say is that one thing about my behaviour is that it is very segmented. All the jobs I've done, I've never behaved like that.
>
> Therapist: You only demonstrate this in your relationship?
>
> David: I've always worked when in excruciating pain. I put up with a lot of nonsense at work I wouldn't dream of—I only once lost my temper at work, I did a "dance of hate" in the car park and I thought, "Oh my God, I have done it in the wrong place".

This new description brings into question the belief in "madness" and invites ideas about what function this belief might have. Judy now declares that she is frightened of David's anger.

Challenging the belief/idea that David might be mad enables issues of responsibility for behaviour to be addressed, and Judy moves from feeling she can live with "madness" to challenging David's behaviour that makes her fearful.

Female assertiveness

Judy reports that David has been different and much less angry. In response to this, David says nothing is different.

The therapist goes on to explore with the couple their relationships with their families of origin. David has a very difficult relationship with his father, to whom he is not speaking, having experienced him as cruel during his adolescence and when he was seriously ill. David discusses how he always kept his adolescent disagreements with his father secret, which he said was the only way he could rebel. In this context, the therapist reflects that Rachel's disagreements with him, which are sometimes very fiery, can now be seen as valuable difference and something that David has facilitated and might enjoy.

The therapist then raises the question with the parents about whether it is Rachel who can be the one who more openly expresses female assertiveness and takes her father on in battle, while it is her mother who has to remain more secretive. In this way, perhaps, Rachel is challenging both the idea of father's fragility/threateningness and that of her mother's non-assertiveness, which she also challenges by confronting her mother very directly. Rachel seems to hold different perspectives about both her parents.

The belief in the need for protection

David returns to the next session worrying that he may be having a relapse of his illness and that his rituals are returning. The therapist asks the couple to take part in a team "ritual", in which she and the couple would listen to the team's reflections on the family's situation and the therapy. At this point the therapist wants to bring in some other perspectives and finds it increasingly difficult to do so herself. David becomes extremely anxious at this suggestion and initially refuses. The therapist decides to persist, and eventually the couple agree. Behind the screen with the therapist, watching the team in the therapy room have their discussion, David puts his fingers in his ears, saying that he does not want to hear anything that is said. Judy listens intently.

Afterwards, what seemed important in this session was not the content of the team's discussion, which in any case David chose not to hear, but the fact that David's rituals had not organized the structure of the session and Judy had chosen to listen to the team rather than attend to David behind the screen. It seemed that this had challenged the belief that David needed special protection at these times.

Following this session, Judy says she has become much less worried and does not feel she has to keep an eye on David so much. The couple seem freer to think about alternatives. Judy's father becomes very ill, and David is very supportive of her, which the couple note as a significant difference.

Gender and specialness

Judy goes on holiday with Rachel, and David describes missing her intensely while she is away. The therapist becomes curious about how they have managed to keep such a passionate connection over twenty years of marriage. The couple both agree that they have an intense marital tie and that they both know that they will always stay together. This intensity is further examined in explicit gender terms, as Judy describes wanting to develop other relationships.

> Judy: We don't have any community . . . (*tearful*). No one ever comes.
>
> Therapist: Would you want more connection with some kind of community?
>
> Judy: We have chosen not to have friends over in the way other people do. And I lost two friends, partly through David.
>
> Therapist: Can Judy get connected to other people if David does not?

David: I'm very affected by Judy's mood. I don't want anyone else around. I don't feel the need for anyone else.

Therapist: Is that to do with being a man more, or being the person you are in the family you grew up in?

David: I've got Judy and Rachel. That's all I want.

Therapist: Do you think Judy wanting to be connected up more is to do with her as a woman or her personally?

David: She's more gregarious.

(Judy talks about other couples she knows where the men use their partners as their "life line" and rely on them to make friendships.)

The therapist tells David that her male team member thinks he has been so demanding and dependent to make Judy feel wanted; however, that she herself thinks that as a man he would more likely want to have Judy to himself. In response to this, Judy says that she is becoming aware of how important it has been to her to be seen as special, and how she has made the relationship the most important thing in her life. This makes her aware of things she has chosen not to do and would now like to develop. The therapist then explores with David what he might need to do to keep Judy engaged and interested in him instead of just being ill or bullying her. David becomes very engaged with this question.

To end or continue therapy

At the next session, both David and Judy report that their already improved relationship has now changed very much for the better. There is some discussion about regrets that the change did not happen earlier. David is clear that he now wants to finish the therapy, saying that he doesn't want to change anymore. Judy does not really agree but does not say that she wants to continue. The therapist has the idea that Judy wants to develop more for herself both within and outside this relationship but that she is constrained from saying this by David's view and injunctions against asking things for herself. This connects to a more general hypothesis that while men come wanting problems solved, women are often seeking "second-order change", a change in premise and narrative, as well as behaviour (Burck & Daniel, 1990).

Because the therapist has started to believe this very strongly, she decides to present this to the couple, at the end of this session, as her dilemma as a therapist.

> Therapist: I have been feeling like I wanted to push the two of you in this session, and I had to talk to my colleagues about this. I had the idea that you are at quite an interesting point. The changes that you have made between the two of you have not unbalanced your relationship, and you have done a lot of things quite differently. However, in this session I began to feel that you are on the brink of doing something quite different.
>
> David: I think we're getting on quite well now. I feel very happy.
>
> Judy (*looks down*): Uh-huh.
>
> Therapist: I have a view that there may be tension. In a way things are very settled and quite different. For Judy, that brings up regrets about things (i.e. not having changed earlier, what was missed by not changing earlier), as you discussed today. But I also wondered whether there might not be for both of you in different ways things brought up about where you want to get to?
>
> David: I don't really want to go anywhere, as far as I know.
>
> Therapist: Yes. It may be to do with me wanting to push you somewhere that you have no need to go.
>
> David: This is a much more stable unit—don't you think so, Judy?
>
> Judy (*looks down*): Uh-huh.
>
> David: I don't like it when Judy kind of, doesn't wholeheartedly—I think it's really quite good now,—when she says uh-huh, not yes.
>
> Therapist: I started to get a sense of a direction I wanted you to take—and that is not helpful.
>
> Judy: What? where?

Therapist: But I think that may be my idea and not your idea.

Judy: Do you mean in material ways, having more friends, more fun.

David: No!! No!! I don't want change.

(*Although David takes this position, Judy says she wants to continue in therapy and David agrees.*)

*Developing empathy
and defining the context of uncertainty*

As David's concerns had been quite central in therapy, as they had in the family, it seemed useful to engage Judy more in thinking about how experiences of herself contributed to their relationship. As we begin to explore her story, Judy finds it difficult to think about her experience, she says she does not know what she thinks or what has really happened in her family. David says he believes that he has no way of understanding Judy and that he is "not emotionally generous".

Judy's confusion about herself and what to believe about her relationships and her experience prompts the therapist to engage David in helping Judy with the task of unraveling some of these experiences. This avoids Judy going into more of a panic and confusion about herself and, at the same time, challenges David's view that he "does not really know Judy".

A series of questions are addressed to David. These invite him not to "define" Judy's experience, which would repeat the original premise of their relationship, but to explore ideas about why and how his wife had developed such an uncertain sense of herself. David describes vividly the ways in which the "official" story of security and safety in Judy's family was contradicted by experiences of unreliability and unpredictability, related in particular to her mother's breakdowns and how these were handled in the family. A description emerged of a family context in which there were many contradictory experiences without a sense of how to validate these. In clarifying this context, Judy's sense of uncertainty and confusion starts to make sense, and she begins to describe some of her own experiences. At the same time, David demonstrates that he is able to think about Judy in a way that he may have kept secret because of traditional gender constraints.

The therapist asks whether the couple will continue these conversations themselves.

> David: We're not very good at talking about these things. The only time we've talked about them is now. I can't imagine . . . perhaps in the immediate aftermath . . . I don't think we could do that.
>
> Therapist: If you thought it was important for you and Judy to talk more about these things?
>
> David: I don't think we're capable of doing that. Because she would always close up much earlier even if I could do that.
>
> Therapist: And you've always taken that as a message to back off?
>
> David: Oh yeah . . . or if it continued, it would continue acrimoniously and there would be no point. Anyway I wouldn't like to do that, you see. I wouldn't want to open up insecurities in Judy, because I need her to be strong.
>
> Therapist (*to Judy*): Do you think there would be advantages for David if you could get to more of those unsaid things?
>
> Judy (*long pause*): I don't know, because some of those things are unsaid because I feel I'm protecting him.
>
> David: I wouldn't want to stop that.

At the same time as David and Judy notice the change in the session, David declares his reluctance to give up his place as the one who needs looking after. The therapist ends this session by reflecting that what seems to have happened in their relationship was that Judy had been giving messages not to pursue the unsaid and David had been very observant. Judy responds by saying: "It's been very convenient all these years to have someone to carry on looking after, I suppose, it stops you looking at yourself . . . I just wish I'd done it earlier."

This session became transformative for their relationship. David, in contradiction to his belief, shows enormous sensitivity to Judy's predicament, both demonstrating and developing his "empathy".

This enables Judy to rewrite her own story, becoming clearer about the constraints she has experienced in trying to define herself and her own needs, as well as constructing through the process, a different story of their relationship.

From this point, David becomes more ironic about his wish to retain control.

> Therapist: How does Judy know when it's helpful to listen to you and take your view as a different view? When it's helpful to hang on to her own view?
>
> David: I have this desire for her to see the world as I see it and not to question that. Once I've pontificated about that, that's that.
>
> Therapist: What's the effect on you when you change your view as a result of what other people say.
>
> David: I enjoy it . . . but it doesn't happen very often!

Finishing Therapy

Judy was involved in a serious car accident, which was somebody else's fault. This became a marker for the whole family of how much they had changed. Despite this reminder of dangers in life, Rachel showed none of her old fears or anxieties. David made an attempt to keep his own vulnerability and response to the accident central, but this no longer had its previous effect. Judy demonstrated her vulnerability and asked for support for herself. We agreed to end the work.

David, having taken on responsibility for his effect on others, was managing his illness and "depression" in a very different way, protecting both Judy and Rachel from this. The couple no longer had bitter arguments in the way they did when they came to therapy. Identifying the context that had led to her uncertainty had moved Judy to a position where she could explore and enjoy new perspectives of herself and she had enrolled to begin an M.A. The atmosphere of secretiveness and risk had dissolved, and David said they wanted to go on to develop things further themselves.

* * *

In this therapy, the family were invited to explore the premises and beliefs that shaped the family stories and interactions. In keeping a connection to societal gender premises, as context both for the family and for the therapy, the therapist and family were able to open up spaces through which a different story and a more mutually empathic relationship were developed.

THERAPEUTIC STANCE

In both these examples of work we use a therapeutic stance that draws on hypotheses at a social as well as a relational level. We interweave our ideas about gender, which are often at a more general level, with a particular attention to individuals' experiences and familial contexts. Keeping gender as a central theme in our work often does not involve explicit discussion about gender as such with families, but does enable us to tap into family stories that contain powerful gendered messages. In each of these cases this facilitated the family and the therapist to re-examine these from different perspectives. Being aware of common gendered patterns also allows us as therapists to notice and question these rather than just participate in them. We are particularly interested in individuals' resistance to and transformation of gendered premises and usually explore these further with family members, as they often provide alternative solutions and viewpoints that are helpful. As women therapists we find, particularly when working with women on their own, that we often use our experience of women's humour to shift context. Paying attention to different contexts has been particularly useful to us as therapists in relation to many themes, but this is especially so in enabling individuals and families to become more self-reflexive about aspects of their societal context that shape them and their relationships.

CHAPTER 8

Training and supervision: addressing the context of gender

As we have become more involved in exploring the constraints and dilemmas of gendered experience in our therapeutic work, so we have been increasingly concerned with how we address these issues in our teaching.

Some of the processes we have been through in each context are similar. In both therapy and teaching, we found that "raising gender awareness" was initially concerned with highlighting the difference between men's and women's ways of expressing themselves and their different positions in a patriarchal society, and with finding ways of doing therapy that reflected a more "female" stance (Burck & Daniel, 1990). As we have argued throughout this book, bringing in a gender perspective when it was absent meant defining gender differences more rigidly than we would now care to. In training, as in therapy, the more we encountered systems we saw as rigidly gendered and oppressive, or behaviour that we experienced as downright sexist, the more at risk we were of being drawn into a fixed position and becoming prescriptive.

When we first started teaching about gender and family therapy, we found that people would often come to our workshops with a stereotyped view of us as "feminists", which might, for example, lead men to feel they were going to be blamed or attacked. This could lead to statements from participants such as "women are the ones with all the power" or continual complaints that we were generalizing. On our worst days, we would feel we had been misunderstood and that we had to justify our position. Nowadays we try to be interested in how such views have developed and use our irritation or defensiveness as process information and not as a sign that course participants had not "got the message". As a last resort, it can be useful to reframe a particularly critical person as helping us to avoid complacency about change!

When gender has been marginalized in family therapy training—and a survey by Coleman et al. (1990) of major training programmes in the United States, Canada, and Europe found that it generally has been—it is very tempting to develop set formats for how trainers ought to address it. If accreditation bodies monitor how training programmes bring race and gender dimensions into their programmes (e.g. the Central Council for Education and Training in Social Work guidelines on training in anti-racist practice), this constitutes a powerful intervention to those Institutes or courses that would otherwise confine themselves to platitudes and good intentions. However, such obligations can bring with them dilemmas for trainers if they feel bound to do things in a particular way, because it may prevent them from creating a context in which ideas and beliefs about gender can be explored openly and risks can be taken without being too organized by political correctness.

We have found it a challenge to develop ways of bringing gender into training which are both powerful enough to make a difference, but also avoid being overly prescriptive and thus failing to utilize those aspects of systemic thinking and practice which are most effective in encouraging people to question their own beliefs and assumptions. Our teaching also continually needs to change because trainees in family therapy have a very different level of gender awareness now than they did ten years ago.

We are concerned not only to teach in a way that raises awareness of the gender dimension for families and family therapists, but also to understand how gender forms part of the process of teaching and clinical supervision. The training contexts we refer to here are those of family therapy training, although some of the issues raised may well be applicable in other contexts.

In this chapter, we address training issues at two different but interrelated levels. We explore some of the contextual issues for men and women trainees and their trainers and how these can create dilemmas in the learning–teaching process, and we describe ways in which we have thought about gender and these dilemmas in clinical training programmes and some of the ways we have addressed them.

DILEMMAS FOR MEN AND WOMEN AS TRAINEES AND TRAINERS

Trainees

While it is important to acknowledge that patterns of learning relate to many different contexts, gender being only one (race, culture, class, education, family, professional, and agency background are others), it is nevertheless useful to think about what might be specific issues for women and men as they enter training. What we describe here are only some patterns we have noticed; they are not invariables nor indeed the only patterns. Hopefully, it will invite the reader to think of differences and exceptions as well as yet other patterns they have observed that affect the teaching–learning system.

Many women who become trainees in family therapy have previously been in a context, both in their private life and in their work place, where they have primarily been organized around other people's needs. Patterns of female nurturance and protectiveness in families are often replicated in the work setting (Conn & Turner, 1990). It may be difficult for a woman to give enough space for the training, especially if she has young children, but it also may be difficult for her to define her own needs. Clinical training creates an opportunity for new self-definition; however, as we discussed in Chapter 3, if you have primarily defined yourself through others, the development of a new professional profile may be a difficult process. For example, we think it is important for trainers to think of the effect of their pushing too hard too soon for self-definition and of not acknowledging some women's sense of multiple experiences, many of which have not been validated in the public domain.

Another issue that sometimes arises for women when they join a training programme, especially if it involves a small intimate group run by a woman, is that this can become a context, often a unique one, in which to be nurtured. If nurturance becomes the most attractive feature of the training, it will be much harder for trainees to take responsibility for their own learning. Other dilemmas may arise if women place the relationships within the group as more important than the development of their own ideas, particularly if organized by ideas of the need for consensus and agreement.

Women who have been outside the context of academic learning for a long time may also find it hard to value their own ideas and become very organized by thinking about what they do not know. Trainers may need to pay attention to and find ways of validating knowledge gained through experience which do not fall into replicating unhelpful gendered patterns. Women trainers, for example, may fall into a nurturing role and be so concerned with the development of self-esteem that they are less challenging of women who present like this. Some of the ideas presented in Chapter 6 about women's and men's discourse are relevant here.

For some men, it may be much harder to acknowledge what they do not know or to experience the sense of confusion and uncertainty that frequently, and often necessarily, accompanies new learning. If their professional background (e.g. psychiatry) has supported a belief in certainties, then the effect on the "unitary rational subject" of questioning these and acknowledging and experiencing contradictions may be cataclysmic (see Chapter 3). They may deal with these by minimizing difference or by clinging rigidly to ideas of objectivity and empirical "truth".

Men and women may, for all these and other reasons, develop different relationships to ideas and also different beliefs about the "ownership" of ideas. Since, in training, we are interested in the fit between what we teach and what trainees want to learn, it follows that we attach great importance to how different people learn, and we invite our trainees to reflect on this too. This is not just an individual, but also a group process, and we find that addressing gender patterns can be very illuminating in exploring how ideas can co-evolve within a group, so that a mode of excessive deference to others' ideas or of competitiveness about whose idea is best can be avoided. Sometimes groups appear to elect someone who will express confusion and not-knowing, someone who will display impressive rationality and knowingness, and someone who will angrily challenge. If these patterns are not acknowledged, they may become rigidified, with trainers becoming symmetrical with some trainees—e.g. those who always seem to criticize new ideas or only engage at an intellectual level. At times, we have found it helpful to inquire whether and how trainees believe their gender influences their ease at adopting a "not-knowing" stance or a facility at maintaining a position of certainty. This introduces another level of reflexivity into the learning system which can introduce a difference.

We see training in systemic therapy as involving learning about learning, both for ourselves as trainers and for trainees. We are always interested in how people appear to have different agendas for their learning and hold powerful beliefs about how they learn, and we try to engage trainees in thinking about this. Some trainees seem to regard training as an opportunity to demonstrate their competence rather than to learn anything new, some learn by trying to link new ideas to familiar theories and claim that "nothing is new", others feel they need to throw out everything they used before and go through a period of confusion and feelings of incompetence. These may be responses to the anxiety of new learning, to constraints from the work context, or to professional loyalties. None of these or other patterns necessarily clusters around gender; however, gender patterns, if not explored, can play a large part in rigidifying such processes.

Trainers

Women and men trainers may also become organized in different ways by these dynamics in the learning process. For example, if challenged by men on a theoretical issue, we as women trainers often find ourselves "proving our competence" at the theoretical level, which may then be experienced as disempowering by those women trainees who believe they cannot learn in this way. Trainers may find themselves teaching only in ways in which they themselves learned best, which may replicate gender stereotyping—some male trainers may find engaging in theoretical discussions with a competitive edge highly enjoyable and thus ignore other ways of learning. "Gender-sensitive" male trainers who are aware of the power issues in teaching a group of women may be so anxious not to perpetuate patriarchal hierarchies that they fail to set up sufficient structures in the training session.

Trainers may need to develop different ways to identify and address their own dilemmas. Training in a woman–man pair offers many opportunities for creatively exploring issues at a process level. One of the authors was invited to teach on a two-day workshop on gender with a male colleague with whom she had not taught before and with whom she anticipated that there might be some conflicts over who was in control of the session. She decided to ask the group at the beginning of the workshop to make a hypothesis about how they thought gender issues would be reflected in the process between the trainers, to observe the progress of their hypothesis during the course of the two days, and to feed back at the end. This proved to be a useful intervention to the trainers in developing reflexivity as well to the group.

TRAINING AND PERSONAL LIVES

The way that intensive training programmes have an impact on the personal lives of trainees and vice-versa has not always been attended to sufficiently on courses. Entering training may be particularly dramatic for some women, who may start to take themselves and their careers seriously for the first time, with inevitable repercussions on their intimate relationships. Sometimes they will be the first generation in their family to have combined a career with having a family, and they may be receiving ambivalent messages about success from their own mothers.

However, as women trainers we may have been more sensitive to the dilemmas for women trainees as they struggle to make space for the training among other responsibilities than we have been to the dilemmas faced by men. As the field as a whole moves to bringing the personal more into the professional arena, there is more explicit permission and indeed request for trainees to discuss aspects of their current living situations, which to date women may have found easier to bring into discussions than men.

However, we have also noticed how guarding against traditional gendered behaviour, such as women looking after men, may sometimes act as a constraint on meeting individuals' needs. A supervisor had a trainee group consisting of one male and three females. She became aware of how stressed the man was at having to meet the needs of a very young family, which made it a constant struggle for him to get in on time and to create space for course assignments. Had this trainee been a woman, he/she might have received far more support and encouragement from the others about the rigours of this life stage and the need to "do something for her/himself". Because this was a very "gender-sensitive" group, the women were especially vigilant about any behaviour on their part which could be seen as over-protective of men.

We have been interested in how men operate in teams where there is a very strong "feminist ethos"; some men have described the effect of watching their words carefully, others have always taken a stance of difference regardless of the issue, others have commented on the way "anti-men" comments and jokes are "allowed" when similar comments about women would not be. In one group, the sole male trainee discussed with the trainer how difficult it was for him to find a way of holding on to his maleness and difference without continually disagreeing with the women, a position that became very constraining for his learning.

We have also noticed that many women set up close and sustaining friendship bonds, which they use as a support to help them through the stress of dissertations and accreditation procedures, and we wonder how far traditional constraints operate on men and discourage them from doing the same.

ADDRESSING GENDER
ON CLINICAL TRAINING PROGRAMMES

The more differences can be talked about, and at as early a stage in the training as possible, the richer the experience of training will be. This involves inviting trainees to think about professional, class, race, and gender differences and to hypothesize about how similarities and differences might affect their learning.

One of us spent some of the first session of her clinical supervision group asking the trainee group to hypothesize about how they thought the race and gender composition of the group (one man, three women; one black person, three white) might affect its process. This enabled race and gender to be raised without making any presuppositions about how they might be experienced. She also asked the group to interview her about her expectations as a supervisor and was rewarded by being asked the challenging question: "If you were a man, how do you think you would be running this supervision group differently?"

Clinical supervision groups are an intimate context in which the sharing of beliefs and assumptions about race, gender, and sexuality can be explored. As always, we have to be aware of the risks involved in thinking in terms of universals and thus, when we elicit ideas about gender, we always treat them as beliefs, as hypotheses rather than givens. We are also aware that there can—especially when the team is working with cases where there is violence or abuse—be an enormous pressure to "get it right". Virginia Goldner commented on this constraint in the all-woman team in the Gender and Violence Project at the Ackerman Institute. She descibes the liberating effect of deciding that "in this room, we [the team] are allowed to say or think anything we want, even if it is 'politically incorrect' . . . we decided we could be hyperfeminist, antifeminist, purely systemic or shockingly linear . . . it was, I think, this freedom to say or think the 'wrong' thing that allowed us to think new things and to combine old things in a new way" (Goldner, 1992, p. 56). Finding ways to allow the unsaid to be expressed in ways that can be useful continues to be a challenge.

In summary, we are concerned to encourage trainees to expand their range as therapists, and this often involves both us and them in challenging our most cherished assumptions, many of which relate to how we view ourselves as men and women. In thinking about issues for trainees, we also need to be mindful of our position as trainers, especially of where we are in our own life-cycle. Thinking of ourselves as part of the generation of family therapists who first raised gender issues in the field may be very attractive to us, but it may also blind us to the unavoidable evidence that many of those we train, as well as being a new generation of family therapists, are virtually a generation apart from us in age and thus likely to be facing very different issues in their personal lives. One of us has vivid memories of a group of eminent American women therapists becoming extremely hurt and upset at an international women's conference when a number of much younger European women insisted that they had never experienced the same sense of struggle and had always taken their equality with men for granted. We, in turn, are continually required to question our own ideas and in particular to learn from the trainees' feedback about the dilemmas they are now facing in relation to gender and how they are similar or different to the dilemmas we have faced.

One main difference has been the effect of feminist critiques themselves. When training courses give gender a high profile, and when as great an emphasis is placed on personal development as on the aquisition of technical skills or theoretical learning, men sometimes express the view that women are better placed to benefit from the training than they are. As trainers, we might be curious about whether this leads to men taking seriously the need to attend to issues of gender for themselves or whether they are worried about losing a competitive edge in a more "feminized" field.

CHAPTER 9

Training exercises

A few years ago, we gave a workshop on training in teaching skills at an annual family therapy conference. One of us commented to the other that this was an unusual workshop for us because we had an equal number of male and female participants. "Yes," came the reply, "this is because it's the only workshop we have given lately which has not had the word 'gender' in the title!"

Workshops with the word "Feminism" in them attract, not surprisingly, even fewer men. Within these constraints, we aim in workshops on the theme of gender to invite participants to expand their thinking about families and couples in two directions. One is outwards, into the wider social system, to think about the impact of patriarchal social systems on the lives of men and women. The other is inwards to thinking about how our constructions of self are affected by the way we have been brought up to think about ourselves as men and women.

Exercises that require same-sex groups are clearly impossible if there is only one man on the course. In general, if we are allocating groups in a course we would aim not to put anyone in a position where they were in a minority of one, whether this were gender or race, because that person is put in the position of having to stand in for all men or all ethnic minorities. However, in many workshops we do not know in advance what the group composition will be; if there is a great gender imbalance, this can be used at a process level, bearing in mind the constraints mentioned above. For example, a sole man could be asked to reflect upon his experience of being in a minority, how it affects his behaviour in the group, and what he could learn about the experience of people who always find themselves as "other". The women could be asked to think about the experience of being the dominant group.

EXERCISES

Gender awareness

Exercise 1
Guided fantasy[1]

In this exercise, men and women are asked to work in same-sex groups and to consider the following scenario: They are to imagine living in a society where biological differences are the same, but gender roles are reversed. Thus womankind is assumed to include both men and women; women are represented almost exclusively in the top ranks of business, politics, the media, the judiciary. Most sport that is televised is played by women and watched by an audience of women, many of them drunk and disorderly. Women commit acts of violent assault against men on the streets, but aggressive behaviour when they are young is condoned as "girls will be girls". Men have been subjected to various scientific explanations about their sexuality, including the "myth of the penile orgasm" and, although women give birth and breast-feed, men look after children subsequently because, having a shorter life expectancy and being more physically vulnerable, it is more appropriate for them to be employed at home while women go out and earn . . . There can be many amplifications to this scenario.

Men and women are then asked to consider in their separate groups what this scenario would mean for them, what the advantages and disadvantages for them would be, and what would happen if they tried to change their position.

Discussion: We have found that this exercise has a powerful impact on both men and women, who of course are faced with the paradox of only being able to consider it from their own gendered experience and are faced with the challenge of trying to be "meta" to something to which they cannot get "meta" (Goldner et al., 1990). We think it is particularly useful to think of some of the advantages of being the subordinate group—e.g. some men say how liberating it would be not to feel guilty and under attack all the time. Because this exercise can arouse powerful feelings, it is important to allow plenty of time for feedback.

EXERCISE 2
Identifying beliefs

We ask the group to get into pairs and firstly to identify six beliefs they each received from their family of origin or community about how men and women should be and then to compare which are similar and which different. Secondly, they are asked to identify one way in which they have tried to do something different and think about the effect of one or more of the beliefs on this change and the effect of the change on the belief(s). There is then feedback to the large group when the beliefs can be written up on the board.

Discussion: We have had the experience of working with groups of professionals from very different cultures and racial groups where there has been a startling similarity between the gender beliefs that people describe even if they are lived differently. Some that seem to come up again and again include:

- women are responsible for children's upbringing
- women are responsible for relationships
- women are defined primarily through their relationships
- men are defined primarily through work
- men are preoccupied with hierarchy
- men are not emotionally expressive

Sometimes people identify contradictory beliefs that operate at different levels either within the family or between the family and the community (e.g. women being seen as very powerful at home but not in the community).

Once people are reassured that we are not expecting stereotypes, we find that they confirm how powerful these and other beliefs are, whether they are still loyal to them or have consciously tried to change them. It can also have the liberating effect of enabling trainees to feel less of a sense of failure about constraints in their lives and to address the dilemmas of change.

A second part of this exercise asks pairs to think about how some of these common gender beliefs would affect women and men coming into therapy, and also affect what they as therapists would observe. Further questions can be posed about common gender premises that underlie violence or sexual abuse.

Exercise 3
Time for a sex change

The group is asked to work in pairs and to identify a time in their life when they wished they were the opposite gender. What context brought this forth? What messages were they receiving from others? What opportunities would being the opposite gender have given them? (If anyone cannot identify a time when they had wished to be the other gender, then they could be invited to think what it was about the context that allowed them to be so attached to their own gender!)

Exercise 4
Addressing the work context

This exercise invites trainees to think about gender patterns in the work context. In pairs, trainees are asked to draw an agency map that denotes gender and hierarchy and to interview each other about such issues as the overt or covert rules that operate about gendered behavior, or any gender differences that are noticeable in the assessment of performance. The questions could also extend to the distribution of tasks in the agency, the allocation of resources, and the relationship between the agency and its client group.

It is often possible in this exercise to draw out isomorphic patterns. For example, the position of social workers is sometimes similar to that of their women clients, i.e. feeling that they carry all the responsibility but do not have access to resources, which are mainly controlled by men (Conn & Turner, 1990).

Clinical awareness

EXERCISE 5
Gendered observations

Trainees are asked to observe role plays in same-gender groups. This can be a useful way of highlighting how gender constructs our observations. One of the trainers can give themselves the task of making a note of any differences in language between the men's and women's groups, between what they choose to focus on or how they give feedback to the therapist.

EXERCISE 6
The gender of the therapist

An exercise that encourages trainees to examine their ideas about men and women as therapists is to set up a role play with a therapist who is given a secret instruction to play the opposite gender. The rest of the group are asked to give feedback on the therapist's engagement with each family member and to comment on what they had learnt about their style. This feedback is then related to the new information that the therapist was playing the opposite gender, and the therapist can be asked to relate the experience of doing this.

EXERCISE 7
Language and gender

An exercise that concentrates on language is to ask groups to observe a series of videotaped extracts from family therapy sessions and to make notes on the language used by the men and by the women (see Chapter 6). Alternatively, a transcript could be presented in which the gender of the participants, including the therapist, is not clear, and the group could be asked to provide their rationale for deciding who is who. The different meanings ascribed to different genders can be explored to reveal assumptions and how these assumptions structure how we listen and what we observe.

EXERCISE 8
Metaphor and gender

Another exercise that explores language is to set up a role play of a couple in therapy and ask participants to decide on a metaphor that they think would fit the couple. They could be specifically asked to think of a "masculine" or a "feminine" metaphor, and the role-play couple would give feedback on how they each connected with the different metaphors.

Clinical supervision groups

In our work with clinical supervision groups, we expect trainees to develop a reflexive stance on their development as therapists. A series of questions that will bring out connections between personal beliefs and professional behaviour can be a useful way of doing this.

EXERCISE 9
Questions for therapists about self

Questions we would invite trainees to discuss in depth about gender include:

- *What kind of behaviour do you find most difficult to tolerate in men? In women? What does this tell you about your beliefs about men and women?*
- *What do you find it most difficult to tolerate in the relationship between men and women?*
- *When are you most likely not to wish to appear naive?*
- *What situations are you most likely to make assumptions about?*

EXERCISE 10
Questions for therapists about families

If the group is exploring their relationship with a particular family, the questions could be:

- *From what you have heard so far, what beliefs can you identify about how men and women should be?*

- *Which of the family members' beliefs do you most agree with? Least agree with?*
- *How does this affect what is happening in the family and between the family and you?*
- *How does this affect the kinds of questions you are asking?*
- *If you were not a woman/man, what do you think you would be interested in exploring with this family?*
- *Again, if you were not a woman/man, what do you think the family would be doing differently with you?*

EXERCISE 11
Questions for supervision groups

When clinical supervision groups develop an ethos of questioning about difference, exploring the effects of inequality on family relationships, and questioning their own assumptions, the trainer knows that she or he does not always have to be the person who takes responsibility for raising these issues. Sometimes the trainer might want to challenge a group about a pattern of always putting gender as the highest level of context.

If groups become stuck in redundant patterns that polarize around predictable positions taken by men and women, or settle into a cosy collective view, then it can be useful to open a discussion on the following questions:

- *What orthodoxies are developing in this group?*
- *How are these constraining us?*
- *What family could we see that would most challenge these orthodoxies?*

EXERCISE 12
Taking on the other's perspective

A further useful exercise here would be to ask the men to argue from what they think is the women's position, and vice-versa. Likewise, if there are particular families that trigger the team to take rigid stances, the women could be asked to observe and comment only from the perspective of the men in the family, and the men in the group to take the perspective of the women in the family.

Clinical supervision feedback

EXERCISE 13
Exploring therapist patterns

When trainees review their progress as clinicians, it can be illuminating to address specifically how they relate differently to men and women in families. One person interviews two members of the group about the fourth member, who is the subject of the interview. One of the two interviewed is asked to represent all the women that trainee has seen in therapy and the other all the men. The interviewer asks questions about how they have perceived the trainee understanding or not understanding them, accomodating to them, challenging or criticizing them, etc. Often very revealing patterns emerge, which trainees can connect to patterns in their family of origin.

Reading seminars

EXERCISE 14
Gendered reflections

We have found that, when running reading seminars, especially where gender is the topic, it can be useful to invite the men in the group to discuss the paper and the women to observe this discussion. The women then have a reflecting-team conversation about what they think the men have left out of their discussion, what they would have said differently, etc. This can then be reversed, with the men as observers, and both groups can share observations about process. Doing this exercise tends to reinforce the general point that the paper is not just to be understood correctly or critiqued, but that the receiving context will influence how this is done.

CONCLUSION

Although promoting gender awareness on training programmes is sometimes seen as the antithesis of neutrality and is reacted to as if it means promoting one point of view only, we find that a feminist position that involves a stance of curiosity about gender patterns has the reverse effect. We find it important to make a distinction between the single-mindedness that may have been necessary to convince trainers and trainees that these issues need to be on the agenda and the belief that there are no right ways to do this. The greater the opportunity that can be created for women and men to explore the complexity of gender patterns in their personal and professional lives, the more this enhances their ability to think critically about such patterns and thus work more creatively.

NOTE

1. Donna Smith generously helped with some of the details for this exercise.

CHAPTER 10

Conclusions and future directions

This book represents a long journey for us, and our ideas have changed many times in the writing of it. It has been very hard for us to stop writing. Our reluctance to finish the text is partly a reflection on the process of co-writing and partly the nature of the subject itself that makes it difficult to conclude. Each time we define a pattern, we question it, the territory shifts a little, and new patterns emerge.

As we have argued throughout the book, when we address gender there is a constant tension between what we call an essentialist position, which seeks to focus on and define women's experience as something separate and boundaried, and a relativist position, which eschews any such categorizations and focuses on a multiplicity of meanings and experiences. We consider that in our thinking about gender we have moved from an essentializing position to a relativist one. In family therapy taking an essentializing position was probably the only way at the outset to challenge therapeutic practices that pathologize or blame women. Noticing how family therapists would adopt therapeutic strategies that fitted more with men's than women's positions led us to adopt therapeutic moves to empower women. These worked very well for some women but did not address the dilemmas of others. When we promote women's positions, we know we are challenging an often invisible and frequently denied set of rules and arrangements that suit men more than women. Feminists have had to shout very loudly to be heard and could not afford to hedge in their position with too many caveats. But in therapy and in our thinking, we consider it vital to transcend any absolutist definitions. When we do not, we know we are getting organized into the same rigid set of binary oppositions that maintain the problem and that we want to critique.

It is probably impossible for us to know why all of our thinking is so organized into binary oppositions. Why do the genders have to be so differentiated?

There is a popular belief that attraction between men and women is based on difference. This, in itself, is problematic in a societal context where difference signifies inequality, and therefore leads to many of the contradictions that face us in our relationships. What are the fears about breaking down this most fundamental binary opposition—and probably the source of all others? Some may be concerned that the genders could become too similar and that attraction and spark would diminish. There is also perhaps a fear of uncontrollable competitiveness if men and women lose most of their differentiation of function. Division of labour has its protective elements, and change towards more flexible arrangements can bring new dilemmas. For example, when couples divorce who have both been equally involved with childcare, there may be more intense and painful loyalty conflicts for the children than in situations where children would automatically be expected to stay with their mothers.

Interestingly, the loosening of the meanings of gender may also spell danger for the force and liveliness of the feminist project. "Contemporary feminist debates over the meaning of gender lead time and again to a sense of trouble, as if the indeterminacy of gender might eventually culminate in the failure of feminism", says Judith Butler (1990, p. ix). The view we have argued in this book is that our current gender polarities actually restrict the expression of difference, and that the aims of change are plurality and equality, offering more creativity and excitement for men and women.

What kinds of relationships would be possible if not predicated on traditional gendered conceptions? Not androgyny or cloning, as some have caricatured, but a range of different experiences owned and lived by both genders, leading to a greater variation in relationship and tolerance of ambiguity and multiplicity. The losses of clarity and certainty that many women and men already experience in these post-modern times could, we think, be better managed if they posed less threat to gendered identities.

However, as Riane Eisler (1987) has pointed out, it is very difficult for us now to conceive of relationships outside the context of dominance and subordination. How do we discover whether patriarchy contextualizes inequalities of power, status, and economic resources—in which case the rigid stratification of our society can be traced back to men's need to dominate women—or whether the oppression of women is a by-product of more fundamental struggles over the control of resources of which patriarchy is only one of many deep social divisions? Does increased power for women always have to be seen as a loss for men?

We find it very difficult to decide how optimistic to be about change. We have evidence in our society of gradual but positive changes in women's position in social and economic life and of slow but gradual changes in intimate relationships, and it is hard to believe that these advances could be reversed. We also have evidence of what many feminist writers have described as "backlash" (Faludi, 1991; French, 1993).

As men and women move towards more equality in some domains or in some nations or classes, would there be new loci for competitiveness? There is some evidence that one sphere is that of reproduction. In many parts of the world, the unwillingness of governments to implement programmes to educate and empower women which have proven successful in rapidly bringing down the birth rate in many third-world countries (Sen, 1994) demonstrates the reluctance to cede agency to women in this domain. In Western societies, the power and ferocity of anti-abortion groups is another aspect of this. Alternatively, as technology increasingly makes possible the fertilization and gestation of embryos outside the mother's uterus, men may finally be able to take control of that most mysterious domain of women's power.

While the battle for control over reproduction is one area where the cycles of progress followed by increased repression described by Eisler (1987) seem to pertain, there are others in the therapeutic domain. One example of how difficult it is to decide how much progress we are making lies in current discourses about childhood sexual abuse. Freud's eventual dismissal of the reality of accounts of abuse given to him by his women patients gave several generations of psychotherapists a respectable means of avoiding the uncomfortable realities of women's experience (Masson, 1984). The last decade has seen a virtual explosion of revelations from women (and, increasingly, men) of their experience of childhood sexual abuse. The potential of these revelations to challenge fundamentally much conventional psychiatric practice as well as many assumptions about the sanctity of family life is enormous. As Elsa Jones (1991) points out, increased rates of disclosure of sexual abuse have accompanied significant advances in women's autonomy and status.

However, some revisionist accounts (Crews, 1993) of Freud's work now focus, not on his abandonment of the seduction theory, but on his method of eliciting stories of abuse in the first place. This has accompanied a great deal of publicity given to "false-memory syndrome", in which accounts of sexual abuse may be fabricated in therapy, especially under the influence of hypnosis. Should we see this as part of a backlash against believing women's experience, giving a charter for the denial of responsibility to abusers and their lawyers, or merely as a correction of some excesses of therapeutic practice? Our view is that we have to be wary of how such popular discourses might connect to other social trends and how they therefore may affect our clients' stories and our interaction with our clients.

It leaves us with a dilemma about how to understand change. As we have argued throughout the book, systemic thinking is a useful tool with which to address the problematics of gender. In our therapeutic work, what we decide to punctuate as a change has implications for the future development of our clients' stories. If pessimism about the wider social sphere interfered with the noting of the small but significant changes made in intimate relationships, we would be doing individual men and women an injustice. Likewise, in the wider social sphere, there are implications for feminists in assuming that something constitutes a change or in assuming that it does not. Identifying and putting down markers of change is as essential for hope and energy in the political sphere as it is in the therapeutic.

REFERENCES AND BIBLIOGRAPHY

Alvarez, A. (1992). *Live Company*. London: Tavistock/Routledge.
Andersen, T. (1987). The Reflecting Team: Dialogue and Metadialogue in Clinical Work. *Family Processs, 26*: 415–428.
Angelou, M. (1984). *I Know Why the Caged Bird Sings*. London: Virago.
Antonovsky, A. (1992). *Acquiring a Sense of Coherence in a Society of Transition*. Paper presented at the Families at Risk Conference, London.
Bateson, G. (1972). *Steps to an Ecology of Mind*. New York: Ballantyne Books.
Bateson, G. (1979). *Mind and Nature*. London: Wildwood Press.
Belenky, M. F., Clinchy, B. M., Goldberger, N. R., & Tarule, J. M. (1986). *Women's Ways of Knowing: The Development of Self, Voice and Mind*. New York: Basic Books.
Bem, S. (1973). The Measurement of Psychological Androgyny. *Journal of Consulting and Clinical Psychology, 42* (2): 155–162.
Benjamin, J. (1990). *The Bonds of Love. Psychoanalysis, Feminism and the Problem of Domination*. London: Virago.
Berger, P., & Luckman, T. (1966). *The Social Construction of Reality*. New York: Doubleday.

Blow, K. (1992). *Commentary on the Social Construction of Intimate Relationships*. Paper presented at the Families at Risk Conference, London

Boscolo, L., Cecchin, G., Hoffman, L., & Penn, P. (1987). *Milan Systemic Family Therapy*. New York: Basic Books.

Broverman, I., Broverman, D., Clarkson, F., Rosenkrantz, P., & Vogel, S. (1970). Sex Role Stereotypes and Clinical Judgments of Mental Health. *Journal of Consulting and Clinical Psychology, 34*: 1–7.

Brown, L. M., & Gilligan, C. (1992). *Meeting at the Crossroads. Women's Psychology and Girls' Development*. Cambridge, MA: Harvard University Press.

Bruner, E. (1988). Ethnography as Narrative. In: V. Turner & E. Bruner (Eds.), *The Anthropology of Experience*. Chicago: University of Illinois.

Bruner, J. (1986). *Actual Minds, Possible Worlds*. Cambridge, MA: Harvard University Press.

Bryan, B., Dadzie, S., & Scafe, S. (1985). *The Heart of the Race: Black Women's Writing in Britain*. London: Virago.

Burck, C., & Daniel, G. (1990). Feminism and Strategic Therapy: Contradiction or Complementarity? In: R. J. Perelberg & A. C. Miller (Eds.), *Gender and Power in Families*. London: Routledge.

Burck, C., & Daniel, G. (1994). Moving On. Gender Beliefs in Post Divorce and Stepfamily Process. In: C. Burck & B. Speed (Eds.), *Gender, Power and Relationships*. London: Routledge.

Burck, C., Daniel, G., Kearney, P., & Mason, B. (1992). *Male and Female Patterns of Friendship*. Workshop presented at Families at Risk Conference, London.

Burck C., & Frosh, S. (1993). *Unpacking Gender Narratives in Family Therapy*. Paper presented at Institute of Family Therapy (April).

Burck, C., & Frosh, S. (submitted). Research Process and Gendered Reflexivity. *Human Systems*.

Burck, C., & Speed, B. (Eds.) (1994). *Gender, Power and Relationships*. London: Routledge.

Burgess, R. L., & Youngblade, L. M. (1988). Social Incompetence and the Intergenerational Transmission of Abusive Parental Practices. In: G. T. Hotaling, D. Finkelhor, J. T. Kirkpatrick, & M. A. Straus (Eds.), *Family Abuse and Its Consequences*. London: Sage.

Butler, J. (1990). Gender Trouble, Feminist Theory, and Psychoanalytic Discourse. In: L. J. Nicholson (Ed.), *Feminism/Postmodernism*. London: Routledge.

Byrne, N. O., & McCarthy, I. C. (1994). Abuse, Risk and Protection: A Fifth Province Approach to an Adolescent Sexual Offense. In: C. Burck & B. Speed (Eds.), *Gender, Power and Relationships*. London: Routledge.

Cameron, D. (1985). *Feminism & Linguistic Theory*. London: Macmillan Press.

Campbell, D., Draper, R., & Huffington, C. (1991). *Second Thoughts on the Theory and Practice of the Milan Approach to Family Therapy*. London: Karnac Books.

Capra, F. (1982). *The Turning Point*. New York: Simon & Schuster.

Cecchin, G., Lane, G., & Ray, W. A. (1992). *Irreverence. A Strategy for Therapists' Survival*. London: Karnac Books.

Chamberlain, M. (1981). *Old Wives Tales*. London: Virago.

Chamberlain, M. (1988). Introduction. In: M. Chamberlain (Ed.), *Writing Lives*. London: Virago.

Chodorow, N. (1978). *The Reproduction of Mothering*. Berkeley, CA: University of California Press.

Colapinto, J. (1985). Maturana and the Ideology of Conformity. *Family Therapy Networker* (May–June): 29–30.

Coleman, S., Myers Avis, J., & Turin, M. (1990). A Study of the Role of Gender in Family Therapy Training. *Family Process*, 29: 365–374.

Conn, J., & Turner, A. (1990). Working with Women in Families. In: R. Perelberg & A. Miller (Eds.), *Gender and Power in Families*. London: Routledge.

Cooper, J. (1990). *Not Just Words*. Unpublished dissertation, Cardiff Family Institute.

Crews, F. (1993). The Unknown Freud. *New York Review of Books* (November 18).

Daly, M. (1973). *Beyond God the Father*. Boston: Beacon Press.

Daniel, G. (1986). *Women in Families: Dilemmas of Change*. Unpublished dissertation, London: Tavistock Clinic.

Dell, P. (1989). Violence and the Systemic View: The Problem of Power. *Family Process*, 28: 1–14.

Derrida, J. (1967). *De La Grammatologie*. Paris: Minuit.

Dinnerstein, D. (1976). *The Rocking of the Cradle, and the Ruling of the World*. New York: Harper & Row.

Dobash, R. D., & Dobash, R. P. (1979). *Violence Against Wives*. New York: Free Press.

Edwards D., & Potter J. (1992). *Discursive Psychology*. London: Sage.

Eisler, R. (1987). *The Chalice and The Blade* (2nd ed.). California: Harper & Row, 1993.

Faludi, S. (1991). *Backlash. The Undeclared War Against Women*. London: Chatto & Windus.

Felman, S., & Laub, D. (1992). *Testimony. Crises of Witnessing in Literature, Psychoanalysis, and History*. London: Routledge.

Ferraro, K. (1988). An Existential Approach to Battering. In: G. T. Hotaling, D. Finkelhor, J. T. Kirkpatrick, & M. A. Straus (Eds.), *Family Abuse and Its Consequences*. London : Sage.

Foucault, M. (1980). *Power/Knowledge. Selected Interviews and Other Writings 1972–1977* (edited by C. Gordon). Brighton, Sussex: Harvester Press.

Fredman, G. (1990). *The Therapist Through the Looking Glass—Reflections on a Systems Approach to Bereavement and A Journey Towards Not Knowing*. Unpublished manuscript, Tavistock Clinic.

French, M. (1986). *Beyond Power. On Women, Men & Morals*. London: Jonathan Cape.

French, M. (1993). *The War Against Women*. London: Penguin.

Frosh, S. (1991). *Identity Crisis: Modernity, Psychoanalysis and the Self*. London: Macmillan

Frosh, S. (1994). Unpacking Masculinity: From Rationality to Fragmentation. In: C. Burck & B. Speed (Eds.), *Gender, Power and Relationships*. London: Routledge.

Gelles, R. J. (1985). Family Violence. *Annual Review of Sociology*,11: 347–367.

Gergen, K. J. (1985). The Social Constructionist Movement in Modern Psychology. *American Psychologist*, 40: 266–275.

Gergen, K. J. (1989). Warranting Voice. In: J. Shotter & K. J. Gergen (Eds.), *Texts of Identity*. London: Sage.

Gergen, K. J. (1991). *The Saturated Self*. New York: Basic Books.

Giddens, A. (1992). *The Transformation of Intimacy*. Cambridge: Polity Press.

Gilligan, C. (1982). *In a Different Voice. Psychological Theory and Women's Development*. Cambridge, MA: Harvard University Press.

Gjuricova, S. (1992). *To Be a Real Woman and a Real Man*. Paper presented at the Families at Risk Conference, London.

Goldner, V. (1985). Feminism and Family Therapy. *Family Process*, 24: 31–47.

Goldner, V. (1987). Generation and Gender: Normative and Covert Hierarchies. *Family Process*, 27: 17–31.

Goldner, V. (1991a). Feminism and Systemic Practice: Two Critical Traditions in Transition. *Journal of Family Therapy*, 13 (1).

Goldner, V. (1991b). Toward a Critical Relational Theory of Gender. *Psychoanalytic Dialogues*, 1: 249–272.

Goldner, V. (1992). Making Room for Both/And. *Family Therapy Networker 16* (2): 55–61.

Goldner, V., Penn, P., Sheinberg, M., & Walker, G. (1990). Love and Violence: Gender Paradoxes in Volatile Attachments. *Family Process*, 29: 343–364.

Gorell Barnes, G., & Henessy, S. (1994). Reclaiming a Female Mind from the Experience of Child Sexual Abuse: A Developing Conversation Between Writers and Editors. In: C. Burck & B. Speed (Eds.), *Gender, Power and Relationships*. London: Routledge.

Hare-Mustin, R. T. (1978). A Feminist Approach to Family Therapy. *Family Process*, 17: 181–194.

Hare-Mustin, R. T., & Maracek, J. (1988). The Meaning of Difference. Gender Theory, Postmodernism and Psychology. *American Psychologist*, 43 (6): 455–464.

Harré, R. (1986). *The Social Construction of Emotions*. Oxford: Basil Blackwell.

Henriques, J., Hollway, W., Urwin, C., Venn, C., & Walkerdine, V. (1984). *Changing the Subject. Psychology, Social Regulation and Subjectivity*. London: Methuen.

Hobson, R. P. (1993). *Autism and the Development of Mind*. Hove: Lawrence Erlbaum Associates.

Hoffman, L. (1985). Beyond Power and Control. *Family Systems Medicine*, 3 (4): 381–394.

Hollway, W. (1989). *Subjectivity and Method in Psychology. Gender, Meaning and Science*. London: Sage.

hooks, b. (1989). *Talking Back. Thinking Feminist—Thinking Black*. London: Sheba Feminist Publishers.

hooks, b. (1991). *Yearning. Race, Gender, and Cultural Politics*. London: Turnaround.

Irigaray, L. (1985). *The Sex Which Is Not One* (translated by C. Porter). Ithaca, NY: Cornell University Press.

James, K. (1984). Breaking the Chains of Gender: Family Therapy's Position. *Australian Journal of Family Therapy*, 5 (4): 241–248.

James, K., & MacIntyre, D. (1983). The Reproduction of Families: The Social Role of Family Therapy? *Journal of Marital and Family Therapy*, 9 (2) : 119–129.

Jenkins, A. (1990). *Invitations to Responsibility*. Adelaide: Dulwich Centre Publications.

Jones, E. (1990). Feminism and Family Therapy: Can Mixed Marriages Work? In R. Perelberg & A. Miller (Eds.), *Gender and Power in Families*. London: Routledge.

Jones, E. (1991). *Working with Adult Survivors of Child Sexual Abuse*. London: Karnac Books.

Jordan, J. V., Kaplan, A. G., Miller, J. B., Stiver, I. P., & Surrey, J. L. (1991). *Women's Growth in Connection*. New York: Guilford Press.

Kaplan, C. (1986). *Sea Changes: Essays on Culture and Feminism*. London: Verso.

Kaplan, M. M. (1992). *Mothers' Images of Motherhood*. London: Routledge.

Keenan, B. (1992). *An Evil Cradling*. London: Vintage.

Keeney, B. P. (1983). *The Aesthetics of Change*. New York & London: Guilford Press.

Keeney, B. P., & Bobele, M. (1989). A Brief Note on Family Violence. *Australian and New Zealand Journal of Family Therapy, 10* (2): 93–95.

Keller, E. F. (1985). *Reflections on Gender and Science*. London: Yale University Press.

Lau, A. (1994). Gender, Power and Relationships: Ethno-cultural and Religious Issues. In: C. Burck & B. Speed (Eds.), *Gender, Power and Relationships*. London: Routledge.

Luepnitz, D. (1988). *The Family Interpreted: Feminist Theory in Clinical Practice*. New York: Basic Books.

Lyotard, J. F. (1989) Defining the Post Modern. In: L. Appignanesi (Ed.), *Post Modernism*. ICA Documents. London: Free Association books.

Maccoby, E., & Jacklin, D. (1974). *The Psychology of Sex Difference*. Stanford, CT: Stanford University Press.

Mackinnon, L. K., & Miller, D. (1987). The New Epistemology and the Milan Approach: Feminist and Sociopolitical Considerations. *Journal of Marital and Family Therapy, 13* (2): 139–155.

Marshall, H. (1991). The Social Construction of Motherhood: An Analysis of Childcare and Parenting Manuals. In: A. Phoenix, A. Woollett, & E. Lloyd (Eds.), *Motherhood. Meaning, Practices, and Ideology*. London: Sage.

Marshall, J. (1986). Exploring the Experiences of Women Managers: Towards Rigour in Qualitative Methods. In: S. Wilkinson (Ed.), *Feminist Social Psychology*. Milton Keynes: Open University Press.

Masson, J. (1984). *Freud: The Assault on Truth*. London: Faber & Faber.

Maturana, H. R. (1970). The Biology of Cognition. Reprinted in: H. R. Maturana & F. J. Varela, *Autopoesis and Cognition*. Dordrecht: Reidel, (1980).
Maturana, H. R. (1988). Reality: The Search for an Objectivity or the Quest for a Compelling Argument. *Irish Journal of Psychology*, 9: 25–82.
Maturana, H. R. (1991). Science and Daily Life. In: F. Steier (Ed.), *Research and Reflexivity*. London: Sage.
Maturana, H. R., & Varela, F. J. (1980). *Autopoiesis and Cognition*. Dordrecht: Reidel.
McGoldrick, M., Anderson, C., & Walsh, F. (Eds.) (1989). *Women in Families: A Framework for Family Therapy*. New York: W. W. Norton.
McNamee, S., & Gergen, K. J. (Eds.) (1992). *Therapy as Social Construction*. London: Sage.
Mead, M. (1950). *Male and Female*. Harmondsworth: Penguin.
Miller, J. B. (1976). *Towards a New Psychology for Women* (2nd. ed.). Boston: Beacon Press.
Moi, T. (Ed.) (1986). *The Kristeva Reader*. Oxford: Blackwell.
Moi, T. (1988). *Sexual/Textual Politics: Feminist Literary Theory*. London: Routledge.
Ncobo, L. (Ed.) (1988). *Let It Be Told: Black Women Writers in Britain*. London: Virago.
Nicholson, L. (Ed.) (1990). *Feminism/Postmodernism*. New York & London: Routledge.
Norton, J. (1991). My Love, She Speaks Like Silence: Men, Sex and Subjectivity. *Melbourne Journal of Politics*, 20: 148–188.
Olivier, C. (1989). *Jocasta's Children. The Imprint of the Mother*. London: Routledge.
Paglia, C. (1991). *Sexual Personae*. London: Penguin.
Papp, P. (1983). *The Process of Change*. New York: Guilford Press.
Partnoy, A. (1986). *The Little School: Tales of Disappearance and Survival in Argentina*. Pittsburgh: Cleis Press.
Perelberg, R. J., & Miller, A. (Eds.) (1990). *Gender and Power in Families*. London: Routledge.
Piaget, J. (1952). *The Origins of Intelligence in Children*. New York: International Universities Press.
Pilalis, J., & Anderton, J. (1986). Feminism and Family Therapy—A Possible Meeting Point. *Journal of Family Therapy*, 8: 99–114.
Potter, J., & Wetherell, M. (1987). *Discourse and Social Psychology*. London: Sage.

Ptacek, J. (1988). The Clinical Literature on Men Who Batter: A Review and Critique. In: G. T. Hotaling, D. Finkelhor, J. T. Kirkpatrick, & M. A. Straus (Eds.), *Family Abuse and Its Consequences*. London: Sage.

Rich, A. (1976). *Of Woman Born: Motherhood as Experience and Institution*. New York: W. W. Norton.

Rubin, J. Z., Provenzano, F. J., & Luria, Z. (1974). The Eye of the Beholder: Parents' Views on Sex of Newborns. *American Journal of Orthopsychiatry, 44* (4): 512–519.

Salt, H., Bor, R., & Palmer, R. (1994). Dangerous Liaisons: Issues of Gender and Power Relationships in HIV Prevention and Care. In: C. Burck & B. Speed (Eds.), *Gender, Power and Relationships*. London: Routledge.

Satir, V. (1964). *Conjoint Family Therapy*. Palo Alto, CA: Science and Behaviour Books.

Segal, L. (1990). *Slow Motion. Changing Masculinities, Changing Men*. London: Virago.

Segal, L. (1994). Feminism and the Family. In: C. Burck & B. Speed (Eds.), *Gender, Power and Relationships*. London: Routledge.

Seidler, V. (1991). *Recreating Sexual Politics. Men, Feminism, & Politics*. London: Routledge.

Sen, A. (1994). The Population Delusion. *New York Review of Books* (September 22).

Serra, P. (1993). Physical Violence in the Couple Relationship: A Contribution Toward the Analysis of Context. *Family Process, 32*: 21–33.

Sheinberg, M. (1992). Navigating Treatment Impasses at the Disclosure of Incest: Combining Ideas from Feminism and Social Constructionism. *Family Process, 31*: 201–216.

Shotter, J. (1993). *Cultural Politics of Everyday Life*. Buckingham: Open University Press.

Showalter, E. (1987). *The Female Malady: Women, Madness and English Culture. 1830–1980*. London: Virago.

Skrypnek, B., & Snyder, M. (1982). On the Self-peretuating Nature of Stereotypes about Men and Women. *Journal of Experimental Social Psychology, 18* (3): 277–291.

Spender, D. (1980). *Man Made Language*. London: Routledge & Kegan Paul.

Spender, D. (1982). *Women of Ideas and What Men Have Done to Them*. London: Routledge.

Spring, J. (1987). *Cry Hard and Swim*. London: Virago.

Steele, M., Steele, H., & Fonagy P. (in press). Associations Among Attachment Classifications of Mothers, Fathers and Their Infants: Evidence for a Relationship Specific Perspective. *Child Development*.

Stern, D. (1985). *The Interpersonal World of the Infant*. New York: Basic Books.

Straus, M. A., & Gelles, R. J. (1988). How Violent Are American Families? Estimates from the National Family Violence Resurvey and Other Studies. In: G. T. Hotaling, D. Finkelhor, J. T. Kirkpatrick, & M. A. Straus (Eds.), *Family Abuse and Its Consequences*. London: Sage.

Tomm, K. (1987). Interventive Interviewing, Part II. Reflexive Questioning as a Means to Enable Self-healing. *Family Process*, 26: 167–183.

Traicoff, M. E. (1982). Family Interventions from Women's Shelters. In: L. R. Barnhill (Ed.), *Clinical Approaches to Family Violence*. Rockville, MD: Aspen.

von Glaserfeld, E. (1991). Knowing without Metaphysics. In: F. Steier (Ed.), *Research and Reflexivity*. London: Sage.

Waldegrave, C., & Tapping, C. (1990). Just Therapy. *Dulwich Centre Newsletter*, 1: 3–46.

Walkerdine, V. (1985). On the Regulation of Speaking and Silence: Subjectivity, Class and Gender in Contemporary Schooling. In: C. Steedman, C. Urwin, & V. Walkerdine (Eds.), *Language, Gender and Childhood*. History Workshop Series. London: Routledge & Kegan Paul.

Walkowitz, J. (1984). Male Vice and Female Virtue: Feminism and the Politics of Prostitution in Nineteenth Century Britain. In: A. Snitow et al. (Eds.), *Desire: The Politics of Sexuality*. London: Virago.

Wallace, M. (1987). *Black Macho and the Myth of the Superwomen*. London: John Calder.

Wallace, M. (1990). *Invisibility Blues. From Pop to Theory*. London: Verso.

Walters, M., Carter, B., Papp, P., & Silverstein O. (1988). *The Invisible Webb: Gender Patterns in Family Relationships*. New York: Guilford Press.

Walters, M. (1990). *A Feminist Perspective in Family Therapy*. In: R. Perelberg & A. Miller (Eds.), *Gender and Power in Families*. London: Routledge.

Warner, M. (1985). *Monuments and Maidens*. London: Weidenfeld.

Weil, S. (1934). *Oppression and Liberty*. Amhurst, MA: University of Massachusetts Press.

Wetherell, M. (1993). *Masculinity as a Constructed Reality*. Paper presented at Conference on Constructed Realities: Therapy, Theory and Research. Lofoten, Norway.

Wetherell, M., & Potter, J. (1992). *Mapping the Language of Racism: Discourse and the Legitimation of Exploitation*. London & New York: Harvester Wheatsheaf & Columbia University Press.

Wetherell, M., & White S. (1992). *Fear of Fat: Young Women Talking About Eating, Dieting and Body Image*. Unpublished manuscript, Open University.

White, M. (1989). The Externalizing of the Problem and the Reauthoring of Lives and Relationships. *Dulwich Centre Newsletter* (Summer): 3–21.

White, M., & Epston, D. (1990). *Narrative Means to Therapeutic Ends*. New York: W. W. Norton.

Wilkes, J. (1994). The Social Construction of a Caring Career. In: C. Burck & B. Speed (Eds.), *Gender, Power and Relationships*. London: Routledge.

Zohar, D. (1990). *The Quantum Self*. London: Flamingo.

INDEX

abuse, physical and sexual: *see* violence
Ackerman Institute, Gender and Violence Project, 126
Alvarez, A., 80
Andersen, T., 41, 44, 90
Anderton, J., 2
andocracy, 54
Angelou, M., 79
Antonovsky, A., 46
authentic self, 36

Bacon, F., 25
Bateson, G., 6, 7, 22, 49–53
Belenky, M. F., 39, 82
Bem, S., 12
Benjamin, J., 10, 11, 12, 28, 36, 46, 51, 60
Berger, P., 24
Blow, K., 17, 90
Bobele, M., 63
Bor, R., 46
Boscolo, L., 7
Broverman, I., 25

Brown, L. M., 108
Bruner, E., 80
Bruner, J., 83
Bryan, B., 58
bulimia, 32
Burck, C., 2, 16, 24, 32, 45, 46, 83, 88, 106–118, 119
Burgess, R. L., 64
Butler, J., 13, 140
Byrne, N. O., 81

Cameron, D., 78
Campbell, D., 90
Capra, F., 21
case examples, 15, 17, 40–41, 42, 44–45, 47, 68–75, 81, 83–84, 86–88, 90–118
Cecchin, G., 3, 7, 13, 57
Central Council for Education and Training in Social Work, 120
Chamberlain, M., 13, 79
Chodorow, N., 11, 12, 14
class, issues of, 5, 17, 29, 31, 39, 46, 79, 121, 126

155

Clinchy, B. M., 39
clinical awareness [training
    exercises]:
  gender of the therapist, 133
  gendered observations, 133
  language and gender, 133
  metaphor and gender, 134
clinical supervision [training
    exercises]:
  exploring therapist patterns, 136
  groups:
    questions for supervision
      groups, 135
    questions for therapists about
      families, 134–135
    questions for therapists about
      self, 134
    taking on the other's
      perspective, 135–136
cognitive development, 27
Colapinto, J., 28
Coleman, S., 120
communicative competence, 38
Conn, J., 121, 133
constructionism, social, 7, 23, 31–32,
    82
  and language, 24
constructivism, 23–24, 26–29, 30, 31,
    32
  and feminist practice, 7
  radical, 23, 26, 28, 29
context, awareness of, and
    acceptance of contradictions,
    4
control:
  within families, 64, 65
  issues of, 38, 51, 53, 56, 57, 141
  by men:
    of relationships, 16
    of women, 14, 38, 43, 55, 57, 60,
      66, 74
  of natural world, 57
  and power, 50, 52, 53, 64, 65, 73
  over reproduction, 141, 142
Cooper, J., 87
Crews, F., 142
culture, 7, 11, 17, 39, 46, 79, 83, 121
  "dominator", vs "partnership", 53

Dadzie, S., 58
Dale, B., 106
Daly, M., 78
Daniel, G., 2, 16, 24, 32, 45, 46, 90–
    106, 119
deconstruction, 23, 24, 26, 30
Dell, P., 50, 51, 52, 56
Derrida, J., 24
diaries, use of in therapy, 87
Dinnerstein, D., 11, 14, 57
discourse:
  analysis, 77, 83–85
  power of, 85–86
discursive styles, male and female,
    86–88
Dobash, R. D., 65
dogmatism of intuitive, 29
dominator model, 10
Draper, R., 90
Dylan, B., 3

eating disorders, 3, 81
Edwards, D., 86
Einstein, Albert, 45
Eisler, R., 10, 21, 45, 51, 53, 54, 59, 60,
    141, 142
empowerment, 55, 59, 61, 62
epistemology, new, 32
Epston, D., 61, 80
essentialism, 36
essentialist position, on gender, 139

false-memory syndrome, 142
Faludi, S., 54, 141
Felman, S., 82
femininity:
  as social construction, 9
  and subjectivity, 38–39
feminism, *passim*
  effect of on men, 5
  and systemic frameworks, 6
  and systemic thinking, 7
feminisms, 21–34, 29
  vs feminism, 4
feminist analysis, and systemic
    thinking, 1
feminist conceptualization of gender,
    7, 9–20

INDEX

feminist critiques, effect of, 127
feminist ethos, 125
feminist linguistics, 77–88
feminist research, 25–26
Ferraro, K., 65
Foucault, M., 55, 56, 61
Fredman, G., 8
French, M., 51, 53, 141
Freud, S., 142
Frosh, S., 6, 14, 24, 83, 88

Gelles, R. J., 64
gender, *passim*
    awareness [training exercises]:
        addressing the work context,
           132–133
        guided fantasy, 130
        identifying beliefs, 131–132
        time for a sex change, 132
    and biological sex, 9
    context of, in training and
        supervision, 119–128
    difference, 6
        importance of, 13–14
    essentializing views of, 12
    feminist conceptualization of, 7, 9–20
    stereotypical views of, 15–18
    and subjectivity, 35–49
    and systemic thinking, 9–20, 49–62
    theories of, 10–13
    therapeutic dilemmas about, 18–20
gendered identities, as constraints, 44–45
Gergen, K. J., 24, 25, 47
Giddens, A., 17, 24, 31, 37, 38, 46, 55, 87
Gilligan, C., 25, 27, 108
Gjuricova, S., 17, 60
Goldberger, N. R., 39
Goldner, V., 2, 3, 11, 13, 19, 25, 29, 31, 60, 66, 67, 126, 131
Gorell Barnes, G., 87
gylany, 54

Haley, J., 7, 49
Hall, J. B., 106
Hare-Mustin, R. T., 2

Harré, R., 80
Hegel, G. W. F., 23
Henessy, S., 87
Henriques, J., 36, 37
heterosexuality, and gender polarities, 13
hierarchies, patriarchal, 124
Hobson, R. P., 36
Hoffman, L., 7, 24
Hollway, W., 36, 85
hooks, b., 19, 30, 39, 80
Huffington, C., 90

intersubjective relationships, development of, 45–46
Irigaray, L., 30, 82

Jacklin, D., 11
James, K., 2, 52
Jenkins, A., 72
Jones, E., 2, 3, 19, 142
Jordan, J. V., 39, 40

Kant, I., 23
Kaplan, C., 25, 39, 85
Kearney, P., 46
Keenan, B., 43
Keeney, B. P., 51, 63
Keller, E. F., 13, 25
Kohlberg, 27
Kristeva, J., 78, 82

Lane, G., 3
language, 8, 77–88
    as constraint, 32
    and gender, 78–79
    patriarchal, 6, 21
    and social constructionism, 24
Lau, A., 18
Laub, D., 82
learning, levels of, 22
linguistics, feminist, 77–88
Luckman, T., 24
Luepnitz, D., 4, 11, 52, 53
Luria, Z., 11
Lyotard, J. F., 24

Maccoby, E., 11

INDEX

MacIntyre, D., 2
Mackinnon, L. K., 2, 50
marginality, and multiple
    subjectivities, 39–40
Marshall, H., 83, 85
masculinity:
    and selfhood, 37–38
    as social construction, 9
Mason, B., 42, 46
Masson, J., 142
matriarch, 54, 59
matriarchy, 54
Maturana, H. R., 23, 26, 28, 29, 50
Maudesley, Henry, 22
McCarthy, I. C., 81
McCarthy, J., 43
Mead, M., 14
Milan systemic therapy, 7
Miller, D., 2, 50
Miller, J. B., 25, 39, 59
Moi, T., 78, 82
mother:
    "blaming", 5
    "double-binding", 52
mothering, essentializing views of, 12
Moynihan, D., 57

narrative:
    approaches to systemic therapy, 8, 77–88
    of self, reflexive, 87
Ncobo, L., 25
Nicholson, L., 29
Nietzsche, F., 23
non-patriarchal societies, 54
Norton, J., 14, 16

object relation theory, 12
Olivier, C., 11
Oxford Family Institute, 90

Paglia, C., 57, 60
Palmer, R., 46
Papp, P., 7
Partnoy, A., 77
patriarchal hierarchies, 124
patriarchy, 21, 30, 53, 57, 60, 62, 119, 129, 141
    context of, and inequality, 10
    impact of on gendered experience, 5
    language of, 6, 21
    vs matriarchy, 54, 59
    value system of, reflected in family therapy, 4
Pavlov, I. P., 22
Penn, P., 3, 7
Piaget, J., 27
Pilalis, J., 2
Pinochet, A., 29
political correctness, 5
post-Milan narrative approach, 7
post-modernism, 23–24, 29–31, 32
    and feminist practice, 7
Potter, J., 83, 86
power, *passim*
    abuse of, 8, 29
        in families, 63–75
        and systemic thinking, 49–62
    and autonomy, 59–62
    and control, 50, 52, 53, 64, 65
    feminist concepts of, 7
    as finite, 59
    historical perspective, 53
    inequalities of, 52
    issues of, 1
    lineal views of, 50
    in male/female relationships, 25
    and maleness, need to reaffirm, 14
    of patriarchy, 21
    patterns in families, 24
    relationships, in society, 9, 19
    of women, 57
        and power of nature, 57–59
powerlessness, men managing, 43
Provenzano, F. J., 11
Ptacek, J., 65
Purvaneckiene, 60

race, issues of, 5, 17, 18, 29, 39, 46, 79, 80, 121, 126, 130
Ray, W. A., 3
reading seminars, gendered reflections [clinical exercise], 136

reflexive questions, 41
relativist position, on gender, 139
relativity, 36
ritualistic behaviour, 106–112
Rubin, J. Z., 11

Salt, H., 46
Scafe, S., 58
science, as masculine force, 25
Segal, L., 14, 37, 39, 46
Seidler, V., 14
selfhood, and masculinity, 37–38
Sen, A., 141
Serra, P., 65, 67
sex, biological, gender different from, 9
sexual abuse:
   accounts of, fabricated, 5, 142
   childhood, 86, 142
   gender premises underlying, 132
   increased rates of disclosure of, 142
   working with, importance of diaries in, 87
Sheinberg, M., 3
Shotter, J., 24, 31
Showalter, E., 23
Silverstein, O., 7
Skrypnek, B., 15
Smith, D., 137
Snyder, M., 15
social constructionism, 7, 23, 31–32, 78, 82, 89
   and concept of subjectivity, 7
   and feminist practice, 7
   and language, 24
social systems:
   non-patriarchal, 54
   patriarchal, 4, 119, 129
      impact of, 5
socialism, 8
Spender, D., 25, 78
Spring, J., 79
Steele, M., 46
stereotypes, 43
Stern, D., 11, 36
Stiver, I. P., 39
Stone Centre, 39

stories, multiple and overlapping, 83–85
strategic therapy, 24
Straus, M. A., 64
structural therapy, 24
subjectivity, 9, 60
   and femininity, 38–39
   and gender, 35–49
   retreat into, 28
   social constructionist concept of, 7
supervision, 8
   addressing context of gender, 119–128
Surrey, J. L., 39
Sutcliffe, P., 55
systemic therapy, 49, 123
   narrative approaches to, 8, 77–88
systemic thinking, 2, 3, 4, 6, 120, 142
   and feminism, 1, 7
   and gender, 9–20
      and power, 49–62

Tarule, J. M., 39
Tavistock Clinic, 2, 88, 106
therapists, women, 74–75
therapy:
   narrative approach to, 77–88
   strategic, 24
   structural, 24
   systemic, 1, 8, 49, 123
Tomm, K., 41, 90
Traicoff, M. E., 70
trainees:
   gendered experience of, 121–123
   impact of training progammes on personal lives of, 124–125
trainers, gendered experience of, 123–124
training, 8
   addressing context of gender, 119–128
training exercises, 8, 129–137
training programmes, clinical, addressing gender on, 125–128
trauma and storying, 81–83
true essential self, 36, 37
Turner, A., 121, 133

INDEX

unitary rational subject, 37, 38, 39, 40, 122
Urwin, C., 36

Varela, F. J., 23
Venn, C., 36
violence, 54, 58, 60, 91, 92, 126, 132
   as abuse of power, 8
   in couples relationships, 65–66
   as exercise of power, 52
   men's vs women's, 66–67
   physical and sexual, working with, 8, 63–75
   and society, 64–65
   therapeutic work with, 67–68
   therapeutic work with women, 68–74
   towards women, 55
      feminist position on, 3, 5

Von Foerster, 26
von Glaserfeld, E., 23, 24, 26

Walker, G., 3
Walkerdine, V., 36
Walkowitz, J., 55
Wallace, M., 58
Walters, M., 3, 24
Warner, M., 25
Weil, S., 49
Wetherell, M., 36, 79, 83, 85
White, M., 36, 56, 61, 80, 85
Wiesel, E., 63
Wilkes, J., 80
women's refuge, therapeutic work in, 70–74

Youngblade, L. M., 64

Zohar, D., 28